No Longer Alone

JOAN WINMILL BROWN

Out of the depths of fear, loneliness
and guilt, a courageous, talented
actress forges a new faith

HODDER AND STOUGHTON
LONDON SYDNEY AUCKLAND TORONTO

No Longer Alone

Joan Winmill Brown

Ps: 34: 1-4

Illustrations

between pages 96 and 97

1

I LOOKED AROUND the furnished London flat and saw a hodge-podge of other people's mistakes. Furniture that had no character. There were no signs of a woman's touch here — I had given up caring. This was just a place to sleep and eat and sometimes, even amongst the terrible emptiness and loneliness, a refuge. Here, I did not have to face people. No "act" was necessary. The characterless chairs and walls required nothing of me and would not talk behind my back.

But the nights were interminable and my imagination would conjure up all kinds of conversations people were having about me. "My dear, she's obviously neurotic. A hypochondriac to boot. Look at her record — two nervous breakdowns. Who would want to employ her? She might let the show down and then where would you be?"

I had once let the show down, when my first breakdown was coming on. My speech had started to slur and I panicked every time I had to go onstage or before a camera for fear of forgetting my lines. Several times I experienced that overwhelming fear — stage fright — when it seemed the audience became some dark monster waiting to pounce and I floundered for my lines and drew a terrifying blank. Finally I would hear the whispered cue from the wings and steel myself to proceed with the scene.

I was playing the part of a bright, American millionairess who was engaged to an Earl's son in *The Chiltern Hundreds*, by William Douglas-Home. The part was based on Kathleen Kennedy, sister to Bobby and Jack Kennedy. The play ran for two years in London and should have been the happiest time of my life. It was marred by fears, doubts and a feeling of never quite belonging anywhere I went. My health collapsed from sheer exhaustion and the author of the play sent me to his family home in Scotland to recuperate. The thought of letting the cast down had haunted me ever since and now here I was again sinking rapidly, and there seemed no way out.

"Dear God, please help me!"

In the darkness of that lonely apartment I realised I had offered a prayer.

My career as an actress had spanned eight years—it had included roles in a number of films in addition to many stage parts and television appearances.

Yet at twenty-seven my life was, putting it mildly, a mess. My health was broken, I could not work properly and nothing seemed worthwhile. I knew I was on the verge of a third breakdown. My complex life held nothing for me and that morning I had read of an actress friend who committed suicide. How I envied her! Her battles were over. Mine were still going on, except I didn't have the energy or desire to strive any more.

"Oh, if only I could escape! I've got to get out of this frightening entanglement. Dear God, please help me! I remembered when I prayed to You as a child, You were very close to me. Now I seem to have gone so far from You. When I see a church I want to go in and kneel and cry my heart out. But I'm afraid. Not of You, but of people. Why? Is it because I have not lived as I should and wonder what they are thinking? When I used to recite the Psalms there

8

was always the consciousness of whether I was being watched to see if I knew the words. The atmosphere of that church is vivid in my memory, for in spite of feeling unworthy there was the beauty of worshipping You. I miss that so desperately. Doors seem to be shutting in my life and there doesn't seem to be much hope left. The dream I once had has faded and I'm left with an emptiness it seems can never be filled."

I walked over to the window. I had often stood there, watching the large tree and envying it too. There seemed to be a peace about it, even though it was rooted and immobile. I dreaded being tied down. The branches swayed in the wind and it seemed content. I had watched the leaves fall that winter and saw the stark bare outline. It seemed to be sleeping, oblivious of all that happened around it. Then, with spring, the buds would burst into leaves once more.

The cycle was comforting to think about and yet I did not see how there could be any new beginnings or bursting forth for me. I wished I could shed all the mistakes of my life and start again, but somehow it seemed too late. Peace was all I really desired now; to be able to turn off the thoughts that never gave me rest.

So many friends from schooldays envied me, for they saw only the glamorous side to my career, not the terrifying heartache and feeling of utter dejection.

Why? What had brought me to this place where I no longer had the desire to live?

I looked down at the street beneath and wondered about jumping. The gas oven looked more inviting. I could just turn it on, open the oven door, put a soft pillow on it, rest my head and sink into a deep eternal sleep. That is what my actress friend had done only yesterday.

The telephone rang in the darkness.

A battle ensued.

"I can't face anyone! Just act is if there is nothing wrong. . . ."

Again the phone rang. I summoned all the energy I had and picked up the receiver.

"Hullo," I said, in a bright and brittle voice.

"Hullo, Joan," came a deep, resonant male voice. "This is John Mercer. Remember we met through my cousin Joy?"

"Why yes, of course, how are you?"

"Fine! Saw you on BBC TV last night and was wondering if you would have dinner with my wife and me next week. We've got some reserved tickets to see Billy Graham and thought we would get up a party to go and see him. Might be fun!"

Immediately I began to act.

"Why yes! I've seen the advertising—it would be a lark to go and hear what this American has come to tell the British about religion."

We made a date and after a few more frivolous exchanges I hung up. I wasn't intending to let anyone know that as soon as I had seen the advertising for Billy Graham's meetings, I had wanted to go.

Suddenly, it seemed as if someone or something had stopped me short. That telephone call. Was it God's way of answering my prayer? Surely He doesn't work that quickly? I brushed the thought aside and contemplated anew the gloom around me.

My mind began remembering incidents of the past, as far back as my childhood. Incidents that had brought me to the frightening and lonely existence that now was my life. . . .

2

UNTIL I WAS four years old my life was normal, except that my mother loved to move and we had three homes in that time.

My father's work required him to travel but my mother was able to give me a sense of security. She was a gentle, fun-loving person who had to face a heartbreaking separation from my father shortly after my birth. He was sent to a sanitorium for many months because of tuberculosis, developed through living in the mud of the trenches of World War I when he was only seventeen. Mother would rise above difficulties with a great sense of humour and meet the challenges as they came. I remember often being bundled into our car and taking off for adventures unknown. Mother was the most beautiful person in my world.

Father was, as far as I was concerned, a giant among men. When he was home the house seemed to generate a boundless peace and the happiness of my parents overflowed to everyone. As I grew taller, my "giant" father turned out to be what is considered rather short in stature; but he still remained a giant in his loving concern for others. This love brought about his death years later, while trying to save someone's life.

The first crisis in my life came when I was four, while

visiting my grandmother's Victorian house near Wimbledon. It had a personality all of its own. The long corridors that led to the rooms, filled with many intriguing objects, were great places for a four-year-old to run and to imagine all kinds of games. My grandparents' dog, Mick, took part in all my escapades and became many different "people" to me. He was a mixture of sheepdog and Kerry blue and I was forever rolling his long hair up in curlers, playing hairdresser. He would just patiently sit there looking absolutely ridiculous. The greatest service he gave me was to sit under the dining-room table and receive all unwanted morsels from my plate while I distracted my grandmother's attention.

The trauma came when I saw my mother's suitcase waiting at the front door. She was dressed to leave.

"Why can't I come with you?" I cried as I clung to her desperately.

"Joan, I have to go somewhere that I can't take you now. It's just for a few days, then Nanny will bring you to me and I'll have a surprise for you!"

My mother had left me before; but for some reason this time I cried inconsolably as I watched her walk out of the kitchen, up the three steps which led to the long hall and the multi-coloured glass-paned front door.

She picked up the suitcase, opened the door and was gone from me. The finality of that scene has lived with me all my life. Eventually I went back to playing in my make-believe world with Mick, but the suitcase still worried me and I wondered where she could possibly be going that I couldn't go.

A few days later my grandmother told me we were going to Aunt Hilda's house. She was my mother's sister. My mother was there and she would have my surprise, my grandmother said.

I was so excited. It would mean riding on the bus, where I could look out of the window and see all kinds of interesting happenings. I hugged Mick and told him we would be back soon and I would share my big surprise, whatever it was, with him.

Finally we got to our stop and I alighted breathlessly from the bus. The walk to the house seemed unending, too, and I chattered incessantly to my grandmother. She was as excited as I was and her kind, work-worn hand kept pressing mine with excitement.

We were at the gate and I waited so patiently for Grandmother to unlatch it. Then I looked up and saw her face. It was suddenly drawn and white and she did not look like the happy grandmother with whom I had travelled.

She had seen the curtains drawn shut in all the windows of the house. This was unusual. My aunt loved the sunlight and her house always shone inside and out.

I was told to play in the garden while Nanny went inside.

As I ran up and down in the garden a little impatiently, I was oblivious of the terrible meaning of the drawn curtains.

My mother was dead. My beautiful fun-loving mother, who had been my security, had died in childbirth. The baby, who was to have been the "surprise", was dead also.

She had not wanted to go to a hospital, but instead had decided to have the baby at my aunt's home, not dreaming there would be the complication of toxemia.

For some time I was not told of her death, only that she had had to go away. Then gradually, as I got over her absence, I was told she was in hospital. I missed her and was always asking when she was coming back. This must have been a terrible time for my father and my grandparents as they tried to shield me from the truth.

One day I remember so vividly sitting on the hard-backed Windsor chair in my grandmother's kitchen crying for my mother. My father took me on his knee and told me she had died.

Died? I couldn't even comprehend the finality of that word.

"Yes," Daddy said, "she died of pneumonia and has gone to heaven."

"Pneumonia?" I thought. "That must be the worst illness you could possibly get, for it has killed my mother. But she promised me I could be with her and now I can't go to see her." I sobbed, feeling my mother had broken a promise to me.

My father could not bring himself to tell me the truth that she had died in childbirth, for in those days, childbirth was not discussed with children.

A year later, on a train with my grandmother, I learned accidentally how my mother had really died. Nanny started talking to the stranger opposite and, not finding the conversation very interesting, I sat looking out of the window watching the houses go by and conjuring up all kinds of stories about the occupants. I was brought back to reality by the stranger asking about my mother. My grandmother glanced at me to see if I were listening, but I pretended still to be looking out of the window. However, I watched them in the reflection.

Quietly, grandmother said, "She died in childbirth. The baby died too – a little boy. Joan believes she died of pneumonia, but actually it was childbirth."

"Childbirth," I remember thinking, "why it must be worse than pneumonia," and a fear of that word came over me that was to stay with me through the years.

3

AFTER MOTHER'S DEATH, my grandparents' house became home for father and me. Some of our furniture was brought there and I would sit alone in the living room, remembering times when Mother had sat in the same chairs or dusted the cabinet and then opened the glass doors to get a book to read to me.

My grandfather—"Fader" as I called him because when I was very small I could not pronounce the "th" properly—was a real character.

He was twenty years older than my grandmother and was waited on hand and foot. The firm of lawyers with which he was associated had gone bankrupt, leaving him with very little money and just a small government pension. But to talk to him you would never have known it. He had an aristocratic air about him even when he sat around the house in his old clothes. His favourite outfit was topped by an old cap with the peak cut off. This intrigued me and I was told he wore it "to keep the draughts off".

He had one best outfit he kept for his monthly jaunt into Wimbledon. I would watch him get dressed and wonder if he were going to London to see the King—such preparations would go into these outings.

His suit would be pressed and brushed by my grandmother. His shoes would be shined to a high polish. He would come down the stairs looking like a very distinguished gentleman—and when he donned his black overcoat, with the velvet collar—placed his hat carefully at a jaunty angle and reached for his black silver-topped cane in the hallstand, I was sure he could pass for a duke.

His white hair and bushy moustache made him look rather like Albert Schweitzer. Surely I had the *most* distinguished grandfather and on such an important mission!

This was kept secret from me for a while until finally my grandmother told me in hushed tones, "He goes to pay the rent!" Their Victorian upbringing deemed that one did not discuss money matters with a child.

He was a great storyteller and when he would sit by the fire thinking, I would wait for him to say "I recollect . . ." This would be my cue to sit on the rug beside his chair and listen to fascinating stories of his childhood in Edinburgh, Scotland.

In the summer he would sit under his beloved Victoria plum tree and count every plum—each day watching them ripen. He would know immediately if one had been taken, and I was usually the guilty party. There would be a mock fight and chase through the garden until one of us gave up.

Fader did not believe in God. He would sit and argue that when you were dead you were dead. There was no heaven and no hell and he couldn't see that God had been too good to *him*. "Not that I believe in Him, mind," he would say.

He did not hold with my going to Sunday school, but my father took me anyway. It was a very dry place and I was always being reprimanded for fidgeting. My friends all got stars and picture cards with verses on, but I never seemed to quite make it.

When my grandfather died, it seemed so very final. I did not feel as if I would ever see him again for I never heard

Fader say anything good about the Lord right up until the time of his death.

I cannot judge, for I know the love of God is so much greater than we can comprehend. If in some quiet moment he had asked the Lord to receive him—even a second before he passed away, then one of the joys of heaven for me will be to see him there.

Nanny was a gentle person. Always working. Always there when you needed consoling. She had had a very hard life. At fourteen she was sent from her village near Thame, in Oxfordshire, to be an apprentice in Hamley's toy store in Regent Street, London. It was hard work and the days held very few hours for a young girl to enjoy herself. She married very young and bore two daughters. There were no modern labour-saving appliances for her. Every Monday, come what may, she did the week's washing in the kitchen boiler. Tuesday was always spent ironing with flat irons heated over the fire.

But Saturday was her big day! For years our routine on that day was as follows: After lunch, which always ended with a suet pudding and treacle "to keep colds away", my father would head for the football match, my grandfather would nap by the fire, and Nanny and I would head for the cinema—rain or shine!

We would sit in the "one and nines" (one shilling, nine pence seats), armed with bags of sweets and be taken out of our everyday world into a fantasy one. Fred Astaire and Ginger Rogers would keep me completely enthralled and when I got home I would act out the whole film. I was determined that one day I would be an actress and get to Hollywood.

With my fifth birthday came the advent of school. One morning, after Nanny had called me, I got out of bed in my usual unwilling way. (I have always been a night owl and

17

still am!) I remembered it was Wednesday, a special day! *Tiger Tim* comic was delivered with the morning newspaper. It was my favourite and the anticipation of it enabled me to wash and dress quickly and come bounding down the stairs. When I burst into the kitchen to ask my grandmother where it was, she could only make strange sounds and try to make me understand by her hands. I thought she was being funny and I made strange noises back at her.

The teacher arrived to take me to school and my grandmother tried to talk to her, but could only succeed in making those strange sounds. I laughed at her and we waved goodbye as I started the long walk to school.

What I did not know was that my dear Nanny was on the verge of a nervous breakdown. The shock of my mother's death had finally caught up with her. Because of this, I was told that I would have to live with my Aunt Hilda and Uncle Hector in Sutton.

I liked going there for visits for I had fun with my cousin Audrey, who was just a year old. But for a regular diet, I was not sure. My aunt and uncle were very orderly people with a strict routine. Nanny, on the other hand, could be twisted round my little finger, to say nothing of my grandfather. With Nanny, bedtime was when I felt tired and I could read until all hours, with all kinds of sweets hidden under the mattress—but not so with Aunt Hilda!

My poor aunt was now saddled with a very unpredictable five-year-old, just at a time when she had enough to handle with a year-old baby. Luckily she had a nurse to help her for a while. The move meant changing schools too, and I was to encounter someone who had a great influence on me. It was the Headmistress, who taught the Scriptures and was a very dedicated person.

Gradually I got used to the routine, but I was always glad when Friday nights came, for after Nanny recovered my father would collect me and I would spend the weekend with my grandparents.

I enjoyed my school—St Hilda's. It was small, but the teachers were wonderful. Miss Cashmore, my class teacher, also taught elocution and from her I got my first encouragement to be an actress. I would enter local Festivals of Drama and won several medals giving readings. Then the school plays were always a highlight in my life. I played Toad in *Wind in the Willows*—dressed from head to toe in green. Even my face was bright green and I thought I must be the greatest Toad that ever lived!

My school required church attendance and there I would sit with the Headmistress. I always looked forward to that. The atmosphere of the church was slightly overwhelming to me when I first started attending, and the vicar seemed to be someone who had really been set apart from us mortals. He was an elderly, austere man and when he got up into the pulpit to preach—I listened. He was a commanding figure in his long black robes and you just did not squirm in his church. I listened, but I did not understand what he was talking about. I knew it was important, but it went right above my head. Miss Godfrey, the Headmistress, had the great gift of being able to make the Bible come alive and so I relied on her to answer all my questions.

The nativity plays every Christmas delighted me. I began as a Spanish onion boy in one (to this day I cannot imagine what a Spanish onion boy was doing in a nativity play, but I have the photo to prove it!). One Christmas I was promoted to one of the three kings. My grandmother made my costume and when I knew my father, my grandparents and my aunt and uncle were all sitting out in the audience I thought my heart would burst with pride as I walked onto the stage to give my gift to the infant King.

19

Next year my big role was Violante, in a beautiful little play in which I had to sing Christina Rossetti's poem:

> What can I give Him, poor as I am?
> If I were a shepherd I would bring a lamb,
> If I were a wise man I would play my part,
> What can I give Him?
> I'll give Him my heart.

It has always been a favourite of mine. I only wish that the last line had had more of a deep effect on me. Although I enjoyed the drama in hearing the Scriptures read and the pageantry of the service at church, I did not realise the full implication of what those words really meant.

Then came another trauma for me when I was ten years old. One weekend as my father was driving me to my grandmother's, he said he had some news for me. My Aunt Hilda was going to have another baby and wouldn't be able to take care of me any more.

Once again the birth of a baby was to change the course of my life and I did not look forward to the arrival one bit.

Daddy told me he had found a childless couple who were willing to look after me and who lived near my aunt, so I could still see my cousin Audrey and play over there often. Also I could still go to St Hilda's School. At least during the holidays I could stay with Nanny and travel with my father sometimes. I lived always in a world of looking forward to my father coming to pick me up to take me with him.

I was given a lovely room in a fine Victorian house. The owners of the house were a very kind couple who tried very hard to win me over. Everything was done to make me happy, but I never felt that I belonged. Once again it was a different way of life, a different routine, and I would cry myself to sleep so many nights. I didn't stay there very long.

In the next house I lived in was a daughter a little older than I, so I felt I would not be so lonely. One day she said, "I hope you realise that this is not your home. Your father pays to have you stay here!" That was a crusher, to say the least, and once more I felt an outsider.

During this time my Aunt Hilda had a little boy named Stewart, who I came to love very much. I loved going to visit my aunt's and playing with Audrey and Stewart. As he grew a little older we made up all kinds of games together and his laughter just filled the house.

When he was about four years old he began to feel tired all the time and his face was always white. I learned one day he was sick and could not play all the games we used to. We saw him deteriorate before our eyes and he was sent to the Great Ormond Street Hospital for Children.

The verdict came back—leukemia.

The full impact did not hit me for I was not really aware of the seriousness of the disease until I saw his life sinking rapidly.

He came home from the hospital. They knew it was hopeless, but my aunt and uncle wanted him to be with them as long as he could.

He kept calling for me, so I went to stay with him those last days. My last recollection of him was the night before he died, asking to be able to sit up so he could colour a picture. He had such determination and although he was too weak to even hold the crayon without my aunt's help, he insisted.

The next day he died and Audrey and I found comfort in each other as the funeral arrangements were made.

We were taken to see him at the funeral home. It was the first time I had ever seen anyone who was dead. But he looked like a little angel and I could not believe that he would not open his eyes and say, "Come on, Joan, let's play a game!"

Audrey and I attended the funeral—our first. The little white coffin seemed so very small amid all the splendour. All I knew was that Stewart would no longer be running, jumping, and laughing with us, and I grieved.

We were told that he had gone to heaven with the angels. Then he must be with my mother and that comforted me. She would take care of him.

With Stewart gone, I went back to live with my aunt and uncle.

4

To a TWELVE-YEAR-OLD who had already been shunted from place to place, 1939 was a year that held even more changes for me. My father met me from school one Friday ready to take me to my grandmother's for the weekend. Just to see my father made me feel so happy and I hugged him before we started the journey.

"Joan," he said, "I have some very important news to tell you."

I was so excited and tried to guess what it could be.

"Joan, I have met someone and am going to get married again."

I could not believe what I was hearing.

"You see, Joan," he said, struggling to find the words, "I need someone to look after me."

I remonstrated with him, assuring him I would never leave and would always want to take care of him.

Then it hit me.

My father really was going to get married again. I saw so little of him anyway and now I would have to share even those moments with someone else. I was afraid and began to cry. Poor father. He had to contend with a child's tears instead of it being a happy time for him. As the days went by there was a quiet reservation, but I felt as if my father would

23

never belong to me again and I ached inside.

The day arrived when my future stepmother came to my grandmother's house to meet me. She was a very beautiful, blonde lady, elegantly dressed. In fact I had never seen anyone quite like her before. Her black coat had a huge silver fox collar, which framed her face. She was lovely, but I hesitated to welcome her. To me she was competition. Competition for my father's time and I hoped secretly they would never marry.

Daddy's wedding day dawned and I awakened knowing that today I would lose him forever. I remembered too that it was also Saturday and I was performing in a dancing festival. My stomach had butterflies galore as I thought of both events.

As I stood on the stage that afternoon, waiting for the piano to give me my cue, I looked at the clock. Three o'clock. Daddy was getting married at that precise moment. I danced as well as I could, but came in second and won a bronze medal. All the way home I looked at it, but my thoughts were with my father and Ann. I felt very much alone. Death had already taken one parent; now marriage was taking the other.

Looking back now I can see how my father had needed someone. Over the years there have been so many things I have been grateful for. Ann did take care of my father. She gave him another daughter, Geraldine, whose love for me and mine for her has grown through the years. Ann gave me a love for literature that I had never known before. She was never without a book and could converse on any subject. Then her love for classical music brought a new dimension into my life which I still cherish today

I now had to divide my time between three houses. But this was to change drastically as Britain went to war with Germany. I was evacuated to my paternal grandfather's in

Sussex, as it was feared the Luftwaffe's main target for bombing would be London and the suburbs. Thousands of children were uprooted and sent to the country to escape these dangers. It was during this time that I first learned what prejudice meant.

I began attending a private school in Burgess Hill, near my grandfather's house. I noticed that the girls were not at all friendly, and only spoke to me if the teacher asked them to. One day a girl approached me and told me she had been sent by the others to ask me a few questions.

"First of all, how long do you intend staying at this school and secondly, were you evacuated by the Government or privately?"

I told her I had no idea how long I would be attending there and that my father had sent me to stay with my grandfather, which had nothing to do with the Government. The look of relief on her face was incredible.

"We were so afraid you had been evacuated from some poor section of London. This is a very good school and we wouldn't want the standards to be lowered!"

What a snob! I despised her. I could not believe that anyone could care about things like that, especially in a time of war. That incident made me so angry and I have carried that anger with me whenever I have seen people suffer the sting of prejudice when others have made them feel a lesser human being.

While staying in Burgess Hill I had my first "crush" on someone: a friend of the family, Phil Norris, who was a Spitfire pilot in the RAF. To a twelve-year-old this crush was very real and I would take off my shapeless hat on leaving the school grounds just in case Phil was home on leave. He said he was going to wait for me to grow up so he could marry me and I could not wait for that day!

Until then the war had seemed remote to me. True, it had

uprooted me once more, but it was not until I heard that Phil's plane was shot down in the English Channel that the devastating horror of war hit me personally. He was dead.

I felt very lonely in Sussex and finally persuaded my father to let me return. The bombing had not then really started in London, so he thought it would be safe for me to come back. However, it was not long before the incessant attack on that city began and it became necessary for us to spend a great deal of our time in air-raid shelters. We prepared food to take down with us whenever there was a lull in activity and to this day I have never been crazy about picnics, perhaps because I had to "picnic" for so long under rather adverse conditions. Nights were spent in the cramped shelter and sleep was not easy as the anti-aircraft guns blazed away and bombs dropped.

It was the thing to show a "stiff upper lip" and so I acted as if I were not in the least afraid, finally sleeping some nights in my bed, defying them to come and get me. But secretly I was terribly afraid.

Once school was finished at sixteen, I could no longer stand the idea that I was not old enough to do something for my country. I applied for the Observer Corps and was accepted as a "plotter". My job was to plot the course of friendly and enemy aircraft in the area, as I received instructions over my headphones. I had to put down on my application form that I was seventeen-and-a-half, and each pay day when I entered the Adjutant's office I waited for them to find me out. But they never did. Instead, a doctor discovered I was beginning to develop an ulcer and he advised me to get a medical discharge from the Observer Corps. Reluctantly I had to leave to a regime of fish, milk and mashed potatoes. I felt such a failure.

To add insult to injury I then developed, of all things, *German* measles!

5

To safeguard against the possibility of a futile attempt at being an actress, my father insisted I take secretarial training. With my mind always on the stage and not on my shorthand I ended up having ten secretarial jobs in four years.

Summer holidays were always events to be planned immediately after Christmas. Working in an office meant asking months ahead for the blessed two weeks I was entitled to. As I changed my jobs so many times, it was a wonder I was entitled to any holiday, but I always managed to work one in somehow.

Joy Elson, a friend from school days, would try to plan the great occasion so that it coincided with mine. We could be released from the monotony of the typewriters that shackled us fifty weeks of the year.

One year it was Bournemouth. We decided to go to the theatre one evening—a decision that was to be an important one in my life.

The play was called *But For the Grace of God*, by Frederic Lonsdale. It starred A. E. Matthews who had brought such pleasure to the English theatre for so many years. He excelled in comedy and his dry humour delighted his audiences.

We enjoyed the show very much and the next day sat on the beach discussing it. We looked up and there was A. E.

Matthews accompanied by some of the cast walking by us. A little further along they sat down. Their laughter kept floating back to us, and I longed to be part of their company. My life was so routine—theirs must have such a sense of fulfilment.

"Perhaps one day I, too, will be an actress and travel and not have to be stuck in an office."

Joy's voice interrupted my thoughts, daring me to get Mr Matthews' autograph. He was very gracious, in fact he asked us to sit down with them and talk. I managed to say I had always wanted to be an actress, and he encouraged me to follow my ambition.

The result of the meeting on the beach was that I started dating the stage director and when the play opened in London several weeks later, I would often go around to meet him and occasionally get to say "Hullo" to Mr Matthews.

One day it was announced that the show was ending its successful London run and going on tour again. The stage director encouraged me to try out for the understudy of the juvenile lead.

I shall never forget the day I had to go for the audition. At five o'clock I walked through Trafalgar Square, past Nelson's Column, and to St Martin's-in-the-Fields, where I had often gone in my lunch hour.

Now I sat there and thought of all this could mean to me. In the quietness of that church I prayed and asked God to help me get the part.

On entering the stage door, I was told to go down and meet the director who was sitting in the stalls and was shown a door which led into the auditorium.

I had taken such pains with my appearance. My emerald green coat, bought especially for the occasion, would offset my blonde hair. My make-up had taken quite a large proportion of company time. Now I was being ushered through the door which could alter my whole life.

Holding my head high and acting as if I were not in the least nervous I walked through the door—only to find, too late, there was a step down and as I fell, a raucous "WHOOPS" escaped my lips, which reverberated through the auditorium.

That was my grand entrance into the theatre!

Two men, who were sitting in the stalls, rushed to pick me up. My hairdo was a shambles. After being told to sit down and regain my composure, which was practically impossible —I felt so humiliated—I met the director.

He asked me what experience I had had and I rattled off as many plays as I could think of, saying I had played in them in Repertory, which I knew to be a whopper. Having banged on many agents' doors and been told to come back when I had experience, I had decided to read as many plays as I could, cast myself in them in my imagination, and dream up a theatre where I had been employed.

After talking for awhile, the director asked me to read. I walked up the steps leading to the stage and was handed the script.

After my reading, there was a lot of whispering from the darkness of the theatre. Then finally the director called me to the footlights and said, "Fine! You've got the job of understudy and ASM!"

ASM? I hadn't a clue what it meant, but I was so excited I shouted, "Thank you," and bounded off the stage with the script tucked under my arm. It couldn't have felt more wonderful if it had been the rarest book in the world.

I was told that my salary was £5 a week (it was less than I made as a secretary, but who cared), and told to report for the first reading the following week.

I walked out of the theatre ten feet tall! The world at my feet. Joan Winmill was on her way!

On the train home that night, I kept looking at the script in wonderment. I raced up to the front door and shouted out to my grandmother—"I'm an actress—I got the job!" She shook her head incredulously and said she really wasn't sure I was doing the right thing. She had heard many stories of the "goings on" in the theatre. One of her warnings to me I remember was "Don't wear perfume, it makes a man forget himself!"

My last day arrived at the magazine office and I said goodbye to the staff. Many had encouraged me in my quest and were delighted for me.

One of the writers on the magazine told me once, "The trouble with you is you don't have any *character* in your face. You'll look much more interesting when you've got some lines."

"At nineteen, who wants lines in her face?" I thought.

His name was Colin Willock, whose name has since been seen on many credits for television. He would find me interesting now—my face is a regular railway system!

The first rehearsal took place in a rehearsal room in a mews near Baker Street. As the members of the cast and stage crew arrived, my stomach began to churn. They were all strangers to me, except for A. E. Matthews (who everyone called "Matty"), as a completely new cast had been engaged.

The director sought me out asking, "Where's the ASM?"

Remembering that is what he had told me I would be, as well as understudy, I hastily made myself known. "Right," he said. "Here's the working script. Put down the moves."

"Moves?" I thought, not having any idea what he was talking about.

The last play I had been in was several years ago for the local church and I had not had anything to do with the stage management side at all.

I was introduced to the stage manager.

"She's your assistant."

"Stage manager?" I thought. "Then ASM must mean Assistant Stage Manager!"

I hadn't the foggiest notion what I was supposed to do, but decided the best plan of attack was to say as little as possible and listen to everything. ASM's should be seen and not heard. Anyway, that is what this one was going to do.

The cast began to assemble and I was shown where to sit, so I could write down the "moves". My common sense told me it had something to do with movements and as I watched the director instruct the cast I realised they wanted me to write down his direction. I had managed to work that one out.

I could hardly write fast enough as he called out to the different actors.

"Matty, you cross over up to stage left and stand with your back to the audience, looking into the fireplace."

This went on all day and when the director asked for the script at the end of the rehearsal his face was a study.

"You did say you had done this before?"

I nodded, scared to death.

"Have you never heard of abbreviations? We don't need a running commentary. I can hardly see the script for your scrawl!"

His face looked like thunder and he shouted for the stage manager.

"Show her the proper way to mark a script and have it done for rehearsal tomorrow."

To say the least, the stage manager was slightly harassed at the assignment that had been given to him, but he tried to explain as patiently as possible to his novice the art of writing down moves.

"The first move should have read—MXUSL (Matty

crosses up stage left). "This way," he said, "one is capable of still being able to read the script."

We plodded through all my writing, abbreviating as we went until it was all finished. I went home rather dejected. My first day had not been the most successful or as glamorous as I had expected.

The next day "prompt" was yelled at me, and I had been so wrapped up in watching the acting I had not been following the script. I hurriedly searched through the pages, but by the time I had found the place another actor had given the line.

Another fiery lecture ensued with a promise from me that I would be more attentive in the future.

As rehearsals proceeded, I found that I knew everyone's lines. This helped if I lost my place in the script, because then there was no hesitation while I looked for my place.

Things were becoming more and more tense at rehearsals. The girl I was understudying was not working out and they decided to let me have a chance to take over the role. Knowing the lines and moves (oh, how I knew the moves!), it was agreed that I could have the part. I was overjoyed, and could not believe that I would actually be in the play instead of sitting in the prompt corner every night, with all its hazards.

The day of departure for Bournemouth arrived. The tour was to open there and an early call was given to meet at the station. As I packed my trunk I remember thinking, "I'm never going to be unhappy again. At last I am doing what I have always wanted."

As we boarded the train, I saw the new ASM busy helping load props, etc., and breathed a sigh of relief. It was too much like hard work and I imagined having to do it every week!

Dress rehearsal was chaos, especially for me. I made my

first big entrance looking like a real glamour girl (or so I thought), dressed in a long black silk skirt and white blouse. My make-up had taken me ages to do, trying to remember all the shading and tricks from school days.

There was a scream from the stalls and the director leaped onto the stage, his eyes blazing. His hands smeared my make-up all over my face, mixing the rouge with the mascara.

"Don't you *ever* appear on a stage looking like that again. You look like a circus clown—and those clothes!" He threw up his hands in horror.

He shouted for the dresser to see I had something else to wear for the performance that night. The leading lady, Joan Seton, was to help me with my make-up. But I was to carry on through dress rehearsal with my make-up smeared "to teach you to be professional!"

Mortified was not the word! Here I was playing the bright, happy, juvenile lead—it took a great deal of acting in that dress rehearsal to keep going.

Afterwards, Joan Seton was very kind and helped me buy the right make-up and apply it. The dresser managed to rustle up a very pretty white dress and the minutes ticked away until "Curtains Up" was called.

I was so nervous. But so was everybody else and that helped. Matty said, "If you're not nervous you'll never be any good as an actress. I'm always scared before I go on, but once I make my first entrance, everything is all right." He was eighty, I was nineteen. So I thought, "Then this must be normal—I'll just hope I can get the lines out."

The call boy knocked on my dressing room door and called "Beginners, please" (for those who open the first scene). I looked in the mirror and thought, "I'm a real beginner in more ways than one, but here I go!"

As I stood on stage, by the door leading onto the set, I

could hear the other actors and my entrance was getting nearer and nearer.

Looking down I saw a large electric wire and socket directly in my path. This would hinder me running in, so I decided to move it out of the way. An electric shock swept through me and I stood completely numb.

In this state I made my first entrance onto the legitimate stage. I had fallen into the theatre for my first audition, now I was shocked into my first entrance!

The play was received very well and I stood excitedly in line with the rest of the cast to receive the audience's applause. It had been worth being bawled out and, with a wink and a hug from Matty, I felt everything was just perfect.

Afterwards we all stood around and talked about the way the play had gone. I felt it was confession time. "Thou shalt not lie" had been drummed into me so much as a child. In front of everyone, including the director, I admitted I had never had any professional stage experience before.

"Strange," he said, "I had a feeling that you hadn't!" But there was a twinkle in his eye.

As I went to sleep that night, my thoughts went back to that chance meeting with Matty on the beach. Perhaps it had not been chance after all. Here I was back with the play in Bournemouth, the place where it all had begun. Its title, *But For the Grace of God*. I remember praying that He would help me get the job—but I don't remember thanking Him.

6

WE TOURED FOR many weeks and in each town I would always seek out the oldest church and often sit there in the peace and tranquillity, imagining the many lives that had come and gone and what their effect had been on the community. There seemed a sense of belonging to see the work of the hands of artisans down through the centuries, who had created these oases amongst the man-made stresses of life.

The stained-glass windows depicting scenes from Christ's life would make me reflect on His teachings.

Realising I was so green to the theatre, the cast teased me increasingly, all good-naturedly. Their incredible tales of experiences in the theatre left me aghast, never really sure if they were true or not. But I figured I was learning and maybe one day I would be able to regale people with such tall tales.

Travelling with a touring company introduced me to theatrical boarding houses. Each town had their recommended ones and I usually left it up to the experience of others as to where I should stay.

I remember one lodging in particular. It was run by an eccentric retired opera singer, who spoke in the manner of the Grand Dame, only slightly "off"! The house was dark, over-embellished, and Victorian, which was advertised as a "home-away-from-home". Everywhere were handwritten notices.

As soon as you entered the toilet, a note warned you—"Do not slam the toilet lid down, it throws my piano out of tune." There was another sign which read, "Pull hard and hold," the toilet being the hanging chain variety of plumbing —circa 1890.

The landlady, dressed even at breakfast time as for a concert complete with baubles and beads, stared at me (arriving late) saying, "You're very late for breakfast, young lady. My good cooking gets spoiled waiting, you know." I often wonder if her large aspidistra plant died after we left, for as soon as she left the room, most of her "good cooking" was hidden under its leaves.

The margarine, not butter, was mixed with cornstarch— "very good for you". Her bath tub was filled with vegetables —"helps keep them fresh". When asked if I could take a bath, she was quite horrified, but finally said reluctantly, "If you insist—but only use three inches of water and put the 'veg' back afterwards."

We managed to fill up on tea, crumpets and jam in little tea shops in the town and decided to take that particular boarding house off our list should we pass that way again!

The tour was coming to a close and everyone was beginning to wonder where the next job would come from. I had not been able to save anything, even though my salary had been raised to £8 a week because I had graduated from understudy. My lodgings each week took a great percentage of this and then the tea shop "fill ups" did not help my exchequer. I must say there were days when I longed for my grandmother's cooking.

When the tour ended back in London I was grateful for the extra money that came in through doing many commercials. Fashions, jewellery, breath fresheners—whatever I could get. I did so many advertisements for different shampoos that I was afraid I was becoming type cast.

Matty had told me he was going into another play, headed for the West End, and asked if I would like him to put in a good word for me to understudy. Naturally I was delighted to think I might be working with him again, especially in London.

The tour had been quite an experience for me. My family had seen me for the first time on the legitimate stage and, most important to me, my father said he was very proud of me. He had always encouraged me to follow my heart's desire, as his father had squelched his talent as an artist by making him go into the business world. When he was bogged down with all the cares of his job he would take time out to paint. In my house I have hanging a beautiful painting of the Mermaid Tavern, Rye, Kent, where Queen Elizabeth I is supposed to have slept. Daddy painted this years ago and I know it was great therapy for him. It is a constant memory of a man who always understood the frustrations of my life but who had to stand by helpless as I made so many mistakes in my search for happiness. So many times I knew that I hurt him, and the thought of this often stopped me from falling even further.

He was delighted when I heard the news that Matty had got me the job of understudying two parts in *The Chiltern Hundreds*. I had met the producers Linnit and Dunfee and read for the director and had met with their approval.

Each day I sat at the back of the stalls making notes in the script while rehearsals proceeded. I was to understudy the leading juvenile role of the American girl and the lengthy part of the maid. I listened constantly to the accent of Leora Dana, the American actress, whom I was to understudy. catching every inflection and going over and over in my mind how she would say each word. After the main rehearsals were over each day, the understudies would rehearse with the stage director in case we were needed in some emergency.

London's opening night of *The Chiltern Hundreds* in the small, intimate Vaudeville Theatre, was the kind of event this girl from the suburbs had never witnessed before— only read about and dreamed of. I could hardly believe I was rubbing shoulders with London's society and celebrities. I was always watching, learning and rehearsing in my mind how one should behave.

The play was a great success. The first-night audience seemed to love it as soon as the curtain went up. Matty was in top form and so were the rest of the cast. William Douglas-Home behaved like a caged tiger throughout the performance once more, only to receive well deserved calls for "Author" at the end of the show. There was no doubt that this was a winner.

Afterwards the cast was invited to a party at Randolph Churchill's. The cast, but not the understudies. Diane Hart, who played the part of the maid so delightfully, smuggled me in with the group. Anyone knowing Diane would not be surprised at anything she did! She has been blessed with a gregarious, unpredictable nature that sweeps you along.

Everyone was congratulating the cast on their performance and there was a feeling of great jubilation.

The next morning it was back to rehearsals for the understudies and I was busy being an American girl one moment and a Cockney maid the next.

Only two weeks after opening night I learned British Actors' Equity was making it impossible for Leora Dana to stay on in the show. She was an American and the part could be played by an English actress who specialised in American parts.

London seemed full of American shows. *Oklahoma!* was

playing at the Drury Lane Theatre and many English actors were out of work.

Leora appealed, as did Linnit and Dunfee, but to no avail. She was given another two weeks' grace and then the part had to be taken over by someone else. Being her understudy I got the chance to try out for it and it was finally agreed I could have the part. Unbelievable. A leading role in London!

Now came a frenzy of fittings for costumes, rehearsals with the cast (many not happy at all with the change or the fact that they had to have extra rehearsals) and every performance spent out front watching and learning until that final night when Leora would have to play the role for the last time.

She was a very sensitive, understanding person, as well as being an excellent actress, proven by the Tony award she won on Broadway later in *The Last of Mrs Lincoln.* She told me she was sorry she had to leave but delighted I would be taking over the role. Somehow I really believe she meant it.

The fateful Monday morning dawned. I was to rehearse the complete play with all the cast and all my new clothes. Some of them just "walked" through their lines as if their minds were far away, which was very disconcerting to say the least.

Matty whispered helpful suggestions and generally encouraged me; some, I think, only just tolerated me.

All too soon I was sitting in my dressing room making up for the performance that night surrounded with telegrams and flowers wishing me good luck. My face seemed to be burning with excitement and my stomach had a whole colony of butterflies careering around.

My first appearance came right at the beginning of the play, asleep on the sofa with my head covered with a newspaper, attired in a white blouse and red shorts — short shorts. This meant having to make up my legs and my hands shook as I applied the sun tan.

Some of the cast knocked on my door to wish me luck and then came the knock I dreaded. "Beginners please!"

I thought back to Bournemouth. It seemed only yesterday my first stage entrance and now here I was in the West End of London! Happiness was being an actress. I had arrived!

I arranged myself on the sofa, put the newspaper over my face and just hoped people would not be able to see my knees shaking.

The overture seemed to go on forever and then finally I heard the curtain going up. Matty made the audience laugh immediately, then the scene started and I listened for my cue. No words would come out, I was convinced. Then I heard Matty saying something about the "playing fields of Eton" and I was sitting up saying, "Say, is it really true they won old Waterloo on the campus there?" My mouth had actually opened and words were coming out!

When the show finished the director came back stage and gave me a hug. Colin Chandler — what a gentle soul he was, I was so lucky to have someone like that.

As I sat in my dressing room taking off my make-up I heard a knock on my door and there stood Mr Linnit, the producer.

"I'm fired!" was my first thought.

He came in and said that, with just a few minor revisions, he was delighted with my performance and to keep up the good work.

I could not believe it and stuttered and stammered my thanks. Then William Douglas-Home, the author, came round and said he approved too.

Afterwards we went out to celebrate at the Savoy Hotel and I felt as if I were on a mountain top.

Weeks turned into months as the show successfully continued. Word would come backstage that certain celebrities were out in the audience and we would sneak a look at them through the peephole in the scenery. One night Cary Grant sat in the second row. I found it very difficult to concentrate for that performance!

Then the Queen and Prince Philip, together with Princess Margaret, came to see the play. There was such a feeling of excitement that night and I found it hard to believe that Her Majesty who I had watched grow up and had grown to love and respect, was sitting there watching me.

Perhaps the most difficult performance was when Queen Mary came to a benefit matinée. The audience consisted mainly of actors and actresses. Knowing Sir Laurence Olivier and others of his calibre were in front did not help my nerves one bit!

No one laughed for what seemed an eternity. We proceeded with the first act trying to be as normal as possible, but wondering desperately what was wrong. Finally a laugh was heard from the box facing stage left. Out of the corner of my eye I could see Queen Mary, sitting there so regally, but laughing delightedly. Immediately everyone in the audience did too. We realised they had all been waiting for her to respond first, a matter of etiquette as it were. After that, the show went very well and Her Majesty enjoyed it tremendously.

As to my own life, it seemed I was always out to some party or dinner. Life was very exciting. Meeting people like Sir John Gielgud and the cream of London's theatre, plus many from society kept me in a constant spin.

What I did not realise was that my health was beginning to suffer because of my lack of experience both on stage and off—coping with my new life was getting too much for me. I started to muff my lines. "Can't understand the girl," I heard Marjory Fielding say one night. She played the part of Lady Lister, opposite Matty, and was an elderly respected actress. She suggested I go to her old voice coach, a lady who lived in Earl's Court.

Her apartment was like something out of Charles Dickens' *Great Expectations* with cobwebs everywhere and a feeling you were entering the past. She was a tiny, wizened old lady, but she knew her job and it was fascinating to listen to her as she explained that every consonant and vowel was like a note of music and we would go over and over a sentence listening for each sound. She made it seem as if we were working on some great oratorio and her enthusiasm inspired me.

But back at the theatre I was getting into trouble with Michael Shepley who played the butler. One night he asked me to come to his dressing room. "You repeatedly step on one of my laugh lines by moving," he yelled. "Get this into your head . . . when *I* am speaking, don't even blink an eye lid. Is that clear?" I nodded stunned by the outburst and as I left, he screamed down the hall, "Let that be a lesson to you!" and slammed his door full blast.

Everyone had heard the outburst and I was completely shattered. It seemed I could take any criticism from Matty because he would quietly suggest a better way to do something and then encourage me to try. But with Michael Shepley I was now terrified of our scenes together. Then I knew Marjory Fielding was becoming more and more critical of my performance.

My dresser Chrissy helped me through many difficult times. She was a warm, dear person and many a night I cried on her shoulder as my nerves began to crack.

Then one night came the frightening experience of forgetting my lines and even though they were being hissed at me from the prompt corner I couldn't even remember what

42

scene I was in. Of course it was with the butler! Then, as he filled in some lines, it seemed I came back to consciousness and finished, but very shaken.

I waited for another dressing down but just got a look this time. But a look that spoke volumes!

Utterly dejected, I began going to a doctor who told me that unless I could rest for a month I was heading for a breakdown. "Rest? How can I?" I thought. "They would fill my part so fast—it would mean the end of my playing June."

So I struggled on, but with the help now of some phenobarbital.

Marjory Fielding could see I was not well and she kindly asked me to stay at her apartment for a few days.

She seemed so forbidding, but under her austere manner there was a generous heart. She cooked meals for me which were highly nutritious in an effort to give me more strength. I had never paid much attention to eating the right foods, not realising how very important this was to me.

William Douglas-Home learned I was not well and offered to send me to his family estate in Scotland for a rest. I shared my fear of not being able to come back in the show and he assured me everything would be fine and not to worry.

So everything was arranged and I was put on a night train to Scotland—to be met by the butler early next morning. When I arrived at Castle Douglas it was still dark. I had imagined it to look like a typical castle, complete with moat, but the family home was a beautiful Scottish mansion, situated in the rugged countryside complete with heather on the hills.

Everyone was still asleep and I was ushered quietly into my bedroom and left to rest. At lunch time there was a knock on my door and as it opened, I got my first glimpse of William's mother, Lady Home.

She was a very aristocratic lady with finely etched bone

43

structure and a regal bearing. She asked if I were comfortable and to stay in bed as many days as I liked. Then William's sister Bridget came in to meet me. She was a delightful person and over the weeks I grew so fond of the whole family.

As I grew stronger I would sit at the window and look out at the magnificent scenery. That was therapy in itself. On the lawns I could see the rabbits playing unheeded.

When I finally emerged downstairs and got to meet the Earl of Home, I was in complete awe of him. I had never met an Earl before. The play *The Chiltern Hundreds* was based quite largely on William's family and Matty played the Earl, so when I met his father and watched the butler serving meals so much like Michael Shepley, I began to feel as if I were still in the play.

"Welcome, my dear," said the Earl. "Do hope you are enjoying your stay."

I thanked him profusely and said I was feeling so much better already—just to be able to sit and look at the beautiful scenery and watch the rabbits frisking on the lawn.

"What!" he shouted. "Rabbits! I hire a game keeper to keep them down." He rang the bell furiously.

The butler answered and listened to instructions to bring his gun *immediately*. He then proceeded to take pot shots out of the windows.

If only I had said nothing. I held myself personally responsible for their demise.

The Earl gave me many moments of sheer joy. He was a wonderful man, with a tremendous sense of humour, but his unintended humour had me having to stifle many a laugh.

On one occasion we were all seated around the beautiful Georgian D-end dining table and the butler had just served the soup. Out of the corner of my eye, I saw the Earl's glasses fall off the end of his nose and into his soup bowl. I could hardly believe it and caught Bridget's eye; she began to laugh too. Lady Home noticed what had happened and said, "Your glasses." "What about my glasses?" said the Earl. "They are in your soup," said Lady Home. "Great Scot," he said and promptly picked them up and put them in his pocket, without wiping them. Lady Home's face was a study and it took all the control I could muster not to completely explode.

In addition to having delightful company to help me to recover, I walked many miles alone over the hills. What a tremendous release it was to me to be able to get completely away from everything and be able to think. Perhaps in my search for happiness, I had missed enjoying the simple beauty that God had created. But there always seemed to be this driving force within me, urging me on—but to where? I seemed to be on a treadmill and there was no way off—for even amongst such beauty, I longed to return to London and get back to the play.

After two weeks we moved over to the Homes' other Scottish estate, The Hirsel. It was even larger than Castle Douglas and I spent many hours exploring the grounds and also the house.

One day we visited the home of the Duke and Duchess of Buccleuch, Drumlanrig Castle, and had tea with the Dowager Duchess. That night they were having a dinner for Princess Margaret and so the Duchess took us into the dining room to see it set formally for the occasion.

The exquisite china and silver that awaited the royal guest glistened amid the magnificent antique furniture.

"If only I belonged in this circle," I thought. "How wonderful it would be to mix with all these people. But I know I don't belong. I don't seem to belong anywhere . . ."

My stay with the Homes was coming to an end and I prepared to go back to London. I dreaded meeting everyone again. It all seemed like a nightmare to me amid such peaceful surroundings. I just hoped the symptoms would not return. At least I did not stutter any more and I had been able to eat normally once again, so my strength had returned.

On arrival at the station the noise of London hit me hard, but it was good to be back again. The stage doorkeeper welcomed me back and soon it seemed everyone was saying welcome home! I ran down the steps leading to my dressing room with a determined attitude. I would not get ill any more and I would not forget my lines. In fact I would give the best performance I had ever given.

It was good to be back and I tried to forget the warnings of the doctor. There was so much to achieve. I did not want to miss a single opportunity that might further my career.

Recently, Diane Hart, who was with me in *The Chiltern Hundreds*, told me I came back very snooty, talking about tea with the Buccleuchs and my fabulous stay in Scotland. William was taking me to dinner quite regularly and this was making her feel quite annoyed. However, one night Prince Alexander of Yugoslavia came around to the stage door—asking to see Miss Hart. The stage doorkeeper called down the stairs,

"Prince Alexander of Yugoslavia for Miss Hart!"

Diane ran to the foot of the stairs and whispered to the doorkeeper, "Say it again—only LOUDER!"

He did and I got the message!

7

DURING THE TWO-YEAR run of *The Chiltern Hundreds*, I was to meet many famous people. But the one who perhaps had the greatest effect on my life was introduced to me by the author of the play.

He stood there with his freckled face and white toothy grin radiating a dynamic personality even in those days. Robert F. Kennedy was then attending the University of Virginia, studying law. Part of his summers were spent in Europe. This was the start of a deep friendship, often filled with many arguments about the pros and cons of England and America.

I remember a visit we made to Chatsworth, the magnificent home of the Duke of Devonshire, who was related by marriage to the Kennedys. Bobby's sister, Kathleen Kennedy, had married the Duke's son Lord Hartington. She and her husband were later tragically killed in separate plane crashes.

Bobby deeply loved his sister and often made the trip up north to visit her grave, located close to the Devonshire estate. It was at these times as I travelled with him that I grew to see the tremendous loyalty and love that Bobby had for his family. He would regale me with many stories of life at Hyannisport.

His mother, he said, was very strict, but loved and revered

by her family. She would not allow them to sing the rather racy popular song, "Everything's Up to Date in Kansas City" from *Oklahoma!*. He would grin when telling me this, but you could sense the great respect he had for her. Her example kept Bobby attending Mass wherever he was in the world.

On another vist to Chatsworth, we travelled up with a friend of Bobby's, George Terrien. They tried to teach me to drive as we went through the villages on our way up North. The scared looks on the villagers, plus the astonished countenance of a policeman on a bicycle, finally convinced them I would need to go to a driving school before I could safely venture forth.

On our arrival we were shown our rooms. Mine was way down a long marble hallway. On either side were statues lining the walls. Some of the romantic period—others fierce and forbidding. In the daylight when I had arrived, it had not concerned me, but when it was time to go down for dinner, I looked out hesitantly. With the coming of twilight the long corridor looked ominously forbidding. In the dim lighting the shadows from the statues were eerie. I decided to walk fast and sang softly "Onward Christian Soldiers" to give me a little courage!

Suddenly, I stopped—listening. I was sure I had heard breathing coming from one of the statues. But it must have been my imagination. On I walked, knees knocking. Then there was a loud scream and Bobby and George jumped from behind two statues and pounced on me. I let out a blood-curdling yell which rang throughout the halls, down to the baroque dining room.

When we finally entered, there were many pairs of eyes upon us but none of us ventured any explanation!

Being a lover of history and antiques, I got Bobby to spend many hours with me browsing through the magnificent rooms at Chatsworth. I have always loved anything that has been made by a craftsman's hands, so when I came to the library with its incredible French tapestries, I could not help but exclaim to Bobby how truly beautiful they were and to think that each stitch had been done by hand.

"Oh," he said, "in America we could turn that out in a factory in no time!" and pretended to be not in the least impressed with any of the incredible treasures that surrounded us. It made me so mad and that started a big argument about materialism and its pitfalls.

But then he started to talk about America and all it stood for and his hopes and dreams that one day all that the founding fathers had hoped for would come true. That there *would* be equal opportunity for all some day. His philosophy was that you did not deserve happiness unless you gave it.

Bobby's friendship came at a time in my life when I felt as if I had really escaped from my suburban background and now could mingle with London's society. The fact that I was an actress meant I had a "passport" to many places I would never otherwise have been asked.

But there were rumblings coming from Hyannisport that my "passport" did not bear a visa stamped with the head of the Kennedy family's approval.

Bobby told me that one night at dinner his father, Joe Kennedy, had suddenly announced over dessert that he understood Bobby was seeing an actress, an English actress, appearing at the Vaudeville Theatre. The tone of voice did not hold tidings of joy and Bobby did not pursue the conversation any farther!

I had three strikes against me, maybe. One, I was an actress.

Two, to make it worse, I was English.

Then three, I was appearing at the Vaudeville Theatre.

The very word vaudeville must have made it sound as though I was a stripper!

(Actually I have never understood why the Vaudeville Theatre was so named, for its past, which dates back to 1870, holds many famous names and plays. Henry Irving made his first appearance on the London stage there, James Barrie's *Quality Street*, Ibsen's *Hedda Gabler* and many more outstanding plays were premiered there. But I cannot find anywhere that it was ever used as a variety or vaudeville theatre.)

Later that summer, I was introduced to Bobby's sister Jean and another delightful person, Ethel Skakel. Ethel's enthusiasm bubbled over as she told me how much she had enjoyed the play. She was introduced to me as a friend of Jean's, which was true. But what I did not realise was that she was falling in love with Bobby. I liked her immediately, for there was a tremendous quality of genuine interest in the other person, and a catching *joie de vivre* that made anyone round her feel caught up in her zest for living.

Although I was playing a leading role in *The Chiltern Hundreds*, I was only earning £14 a week. I had taken over after the first month and had attained what every understudy dreams of, except a rise in salary. However, trying to dress, live and tip all the different staff members at the theatre each week was a difficult task. I asked the management for a rise. In shocked tones I was told how disappointed they were in me—here they had given me my big chance and all I cared about was money!

Anyway, Bobby was quick to notice I was having difficulties making ends meet and parcels arrived with beautiful clothes in them "scrounged" from his sisters. Labels like Saks 5th Avenue, Bonwit Teller, Bergdorf Goodman—I was overjoyed. At least I looked successful in my beautiful American clothes.

Two of the dresses stand out in my mind, A lovely green velvet, cut in an Elizabethan style and a white felt skirt appliquéd with navy, topped by a navy silk shirt.

I wore the white felt skirt ensemble one evening when my agent took me to a party honouring Errol Flynn. He arrived looking as if he had just disembarked from a yacht, dressed in a navy blazer, cravat and white trousers. He was immediately surrounded by a bevy of beautiful girls and I was sure I had seen the whole scene in one of his movies.

I remember sitting on a settee that night talking to an actor—when suddenly someone upset an ashtray all over my white felt skirt. I was mortified. My evening was ruined when, lo and behold, Cesar Romero emerged from out of the crowd, whisked out his pocket handkerchief and dusted off the offending ashes.

It was worth the moment's distress to receive such gallantry!

One night after entering the stage door for almost two years—I saw the final notice on the bulletin board. We were closing in two weeks.

The play and the people had become a way of life for me and I dreaded the final night. Every actor or actress has a dread in the back of their minds that they will never work again. My dread obsessed me and on the last night when the final curtain came down, I went back to my flat utterly dejected. My confidence was sinking rapidly, together with my bank balance.

The play was going to Broadway as *Yes, M'Lord* and most of the cast were going with it. However, because I was playing an American part, American Equity ruled an American would have to play it. This was fair enough—especially after English Equity had insisted a Briton play the part in London. I hoped Leora Dana could play the part again.

However, this thought did not help the cold fact—most of the cast were going to America, but not me. Apart from the idea of not being with the play, I had always wanted to visit America. Broadway seemed such a glamorous place.

The few of us who were left in London from *The Chiltern Hundreds* would meet in a little restaurant off Piccadilly Circus. It was a meeting place for actors and actresses of all strata and was a fantastic hive of information concerning who was casting what.

To go there I would take as many pains as if I were going to Ascot, for you never knew just who you might meet. The actors' entrances were incredible and everyone tried to outdo the other. But it was a place to go and not feel like an outsider.

Because I was so nervous I smoked and to add to the dramatic effect would use a long cigarette holder. I really did not enjoy smoking, but it gave me something to do with my hands and added, especially with the holder, a sense of sophistication which I really did not have.

News of auditions would filter through over tea and I would make mental notes to call the casting offices. Agents who had been interested in me during the run of *The Chiltern Hundreds* were called and each day I waited, hoping.

William Douglas-Home knew I was having difficult times financially so he asked me to do some secretarial work for him. (My father was right! He wanted me to have something to fall back on when he insisted on my secretarial training!)

One day while sorting William's mail, I came across a letter which was opened, and waiting to be filed. It was from Matty. He told of the reception they were having in America. It sounded so exciting playing on Broadway. I longed to be there.

Then a sentence hit my eye and crushed me deeply.

"At last we have a real June—Elaine Stritch is great in the part!"

Matty—who had been my mentor, my idol, was saying "At last we have a *real* June!" He had told me so often how good I was, how pleased he was. Now, my confidence, not only in myself but in other people—hit zero.

I put the letter down and walked out into the street and made my way to St James's Park to recover. I fed the ducks and the swans automatically, for I was deep in thought remembering all the wonderful things Matty had said about my performance. Were they true or not? Could I act—or was I fooling myself?

I didn't want to face anyone and I walked to a telephone booth and made a call cancelling an appointment for that evening. I wanted to run, but where? I felt locked inside my body and desperately wanted to free myself of all everyday responsibilities.

I went back to my flat. Closing the door, I felt an utter failure. I didn't want my family or friends to know this, so again the mask had to be readjusted and the "happy talk" well rehearsed so it would not sound too brittle to the hearer.

The one thing I looked forward to were my letters from Bobby, which came regularly, telling of his studies at the University of Virginia; his many escapades and his hopes to get back to London as soon as he could.

I was dating several men, knowing Bobby was dating in America. But to me he was very special and I believe for the first time in my life I considered myself to be "in love". Looking back now I believe I was "in love" with his mode of life. The excitement, the glamour and needless to say, his financial status. To a girl from the suburbs he epitomised everything one could dream of.

So again I was not prepared for the contents of a letter I received from him in the weeks that lay ahead.

The familiar Hyannisport postmark meant he was home for the summer and would also mean he would probably be heading for London soon.

I opened it, excited at the thought. Then I read, "I am getting married to Ethel Skakel . . ."

I couldn't believe my eyes.

The girl I had met with his sister Jean in my dressing room that night.

It seemed that all my bad news lately came in letters from America.

I did not know then that God knew the future—He was working it out and that one day in America I would meet His choice for me. Elizabeth Barrett Browning says it so eloquently, "God's gifts put men's best dreams to shame."

Bobby was marrying God's gift to him and as history testifies, He made no mistake. Ethel was the perfect wife for Bobby. She has a depth that belies the bubbling personality and a resiliency that brought her through the untold agony of seeing her husband assassinated.

Bobby's assassination hit me deeply and brought back many memories of the carefree boy I knew, who loved life and was anxious to be a contributing factor in helping others. His Irish temper could flare, there was a great obstinacy in his nature, but all these traits were used as he fought to help people who had no one to speak for them.

8

AFTER THE NEWS of Bobby's impending marriage, there was only one thing I could do to escape the feeling of utter disappointment—work. I decided not to wait for the two good breaks that my agent had told me were in the offing and accepted straight off a contract to appear as a guest star in small town repertory companies as June in *The Chiltern Hundreds*.

One engagement stands out in my mind . . . Aberystwyth, Wales.

Upon arriving there, I was told it was one-night stands in the surrounding villages, a long way up in the mountains. Very different from what I had imagined.

Props and cast were loaded on to a double decker bus each night and we set off over winding, bumpy roads to the villages of Wales. "A far cry from the West End of London," I thought.

It was bitterly cold and we ploughed through deep snow to get to some villages. It was the lambing season and I remember wondering why it was that God had so arranged it that a baby lamb had to endure the hazards of the bitter snow storms. It seemed they had enough to do just to survive. But they did survive—another miracle that goes so frequently unheeded.

One little town I will always remember, even though I have long forgotten its name. We arrived at the "theatre"—actually a village hall—ready to perform, only to find the boiler had burst and there was no heat. It was freezing and I had my first entrance in shorts! It was no good throwing any kind of leading lady tantrums, no one would have cared less and nothing could be done about it. That was bad enough, but some stray cats had made their home in the auditorium and oh! how that place smelled.

In between freezing, I thought I would "gag" to death!

My first scene was a battle between laughter and tears as I remembered my West End days. I looked at the scenery. It was permanent, so one had to improvise one's exits and entrances accordingly. The furniture looked like Salvation Army rejects and the sight of the beaten-up settee that I had to lie on turned my tears into laughter. It was so incongruous to imagine that this was supposed to represent the home of an Earl!

The next week we came back and played *The Winslow Boy* by Terence Rattigan in the same set, with the same furnishings. The boiler had been mended, but the other problem—the cats—had not been remedied. (Where, oh, where was the glamour of the theatre?!)

Looking back, I would not have missed the experience of the hardships of a one-night stand touring group. At the time I felt completely bewildered at finding myself so far from the West End of London and the prestige that went with it.

Even then I can see God had His hand on my life. I had stumbled, literally, into show business without any real on-the-job training or experience. It was good for me too, to see how others, who were so dedicated to their profession, put up with hardships. I am glad now it was not handed to me *carte blanche*. My character was, and is, such that I really do not believe I could be trusted with easy success.

Pride raises its ugly head in many forms and when it does in my life God has very kindly put His loving foot in my path and allowed me to take a fall. I guess He will have to keep on doing it, for just when I think I have learned humility and all its attributes—down I go again.

After my stint with guest appearances was over, I returned to London and continued dating John French, an actor I had met. No two people could be more unsuited to each other. But God had a plan, even in this.

We saw each other regularly, but there were many tirades, for each of us was trying to find all the answers to all our frustrations and longings in each other. There was the constant fear, too, of loneliness. Deep down inside I was afraid of the future, afraid of being alone, even though I had many friends.

He basically had the same fears and perhaps our greatest fear was of being failures in life. I believe so many people are drawn together in this way and that is why there are so many unhappy relationships. For it is not based on real giving love, but purely on a need to *be* loved.

We worked together on tours, in repertory and our conflict of personalities made it *Heartbreak House* all the way.

There was a feeling of futility to our relationship, but there seemed no answer—which ever way a decision would be made there had to be the inevitable tearing apart of that which was deep within me.

I kept busy with commercials, TV appearances and films, but all the time I seemed to be fighting a losing battle with my health once more.

When I was playing Brighton again—this time in George Bernard Shaw's *Arms and the Man* in the role of Raina, I was nearing collapse. I was so exhausted and had lost so much weight it was a struggle just to get to the theatre at night.

I loved the part—playing opposite Andrew Crawford—and I struggled on somehow each night. But friends could see I was not well and suggested I stay on in Brighton in a nursing home for a while. The tour was over after this date and unwillingly I agreed to this. The thought of a nursing home scared me and all I wanted to do was to get home to London and rest, but I knew physically I could not look after myself properly. I stayed there for a while, then discharged myself and went home. After I arrived back in London I slept, it seemed, for days, feeling extremely weak. Just the thought of trying to get back to work looked impossible. My London doctor again told me to take great care of myself. Rest, take particular attention to my meals and pace myself, instead of always being active and trying to pursue my career. It seemed as if I were in a complete vicious circle—if I didn't work I didn't eat, if I did work I collapsed. There had to be an answer and I had to find it. I looked at others who seemingly had so much physical strength and I envied them.

After a while I began to find I didn't really care what work I got. Friends would say, "Hold out for the big breaks, don't do any 'B' films." But my confidence was slowly sinking and I knew that when I went for interviews I did not make a good impression.

Finally, I signed a contract to go on tour in *Dracula* with none other than Bela Lugosi, who had created the role in the movie and was going to tour England in the play.

I was very hesitant to attend the first rehearsal and meet Mr Lugosi. He arrived late making a grand entrance and was introduced to each of the cast. When it came to my turn, I stood there in sheer amazement. He looked just like the wax figure of Count Dracula that had scared me so as a child when at a cinema. But he was gracious and very professional as we proceeded with the first reading.

He took playing the part of Count Dracula very seriously

and we were never allowed to change a word, a look or a move. It was as sacred as Shakespeare to him.

Once, I heard him say that perhaps the worst thing for his career had been the success of *Dracula*, for people would never take him seriously as an actor any more. Apparently, he had known great adulation in his homeland of Hungary.

In the final scene, set in a crypt, he was supposed to be in a coffin when the doctor and his friend Van Helsing drive a stake in his heart—the only way he can be killed. But Bela would never get in the coffin and would always give the death scream from the wings. He had a great superstition about this.

The only time we saw him during the day would be when we would meet at the train to move from one city to another. Then he would stride down the platform with his wife and son and disappear into a private compartment with the shades drawn for the entire journey.

The trouble with the cast was that after we got over the awe of being with *the* Dracula our emotions swung the other way.

The overly dramatic dialogue became too much for us and we all started to get the giggles. I cannot begin to describe the agonies we went through every night trying to control our feelings and playing our lines "straight". Once the stage director called us all on stage after a particularly "giggly" show and said he would fire all of us if we did not stop this appalling laughing. Even as he said this, someone giggled and started all of us off again. We were appearing in a theatre way up north of London and the poor director had no choice but to put up with us. It even got to him finally as night after night he had to oversee the fake bats and smoke that always preceded Dracula's appearance.

One night, I came to the scene where Dracula was supposed to hypnotise me, just after I gasp in horror at seeing

59

him. The smoke that was pumped under his cape each time he would make an entrance with arms wide apart, got down my throat and knocked me out cold. The audience was unaware of what had happened and somehow Bela ad libbed his way through the scene with me prostrate on the ground. As soon as the curtain came down I was whisked off to the waiting arms of a St John's Ambulance man.

Bela proceeded to direct all the traffic that had gathered, even to stopping brandy being administered to me from a well meaning member of the cast. "Noooothing by way of mouth," he kept repeating, "Nooooooothing!"

I recovered enough to go on again the next day, but I was very careful not to exclaim too heartily upon seeing Dracula coming through my window.

We returned to London and played all the surrounding theatres and then our tour was over. I was rather relieved I must say. Touring had never been my favourite part of theatre life and now perhaps there would be a good break waiting for me.

As it turned out I landed the leading part opposite Guy Middleton in the film, *The Harassed Hero* — it was supposed to be the beginning of a series, but the catastrophic goings on behind scenes cancelled out any hope. The director was fired a few days after shooting began, a new one arrived and the script was completely rewritten. Chaos abounded around us, but we enjoyed ourselves nevertheless.

Then came more films and life seemed to be going along smoothly. Until then it seemed my health had improved but suddenly I began to see the tell-tale signs that all was not well. My speech started to slur again, the headaches were becoming unbearable and the feeling of wanting to run away from it all dominated me.

I was so tired of always acting off-stage. Trying to be vivacious when I felt completely exhausted. I never seemed able to be myself any more. Perhaps I had always acted—had I built a façade around me to protect me from people really knowing me? The mask was being worn more often now, because the last thing I wanted was people—my friends, in particular—to know the desperation I was feeling.

Where was the happiness I thought I would always have now that I was an actress? I wanted to find the ultimate in life, but where was it leading me?

9

I REMEMBER, WITH an almost cold detachment, the advent of my breakdown. It is as if I can see a scene being played out by someone else, but when I look closely the central figure is me—and I do not like what I am watching. It is a scene I would like to erase completely from my life, for the nightmarish memory of it sometimes sweeps over me and if I did not now have the deep assurance of God's love and forgiveness it would drag me down again into a pit of despair and self-pity.

For weeks I had sensed a feeling of desperation and a longing for peace. It seemed as if the struggle to try to make a career was futile, for my health would so often keep me from attending auditions. When I did, my appearance and reading of the part did not send the producers into ecstasies. My confidence was gone.

I dreaded getting out of bed in the morning and having to face people. The thought of even crossing a street would send fear running through me.

What was happening to me?

Always in the past I had been game to try anything, and had enjoyed the unexpected telephone call that could have me racing out of the flat, bound for some delightful serendipity experience. Now, I dreaded the ring of the telephone.

I looked at myself in the mirror and saw a person who looked old beyond her years. No amount of make-up could hide the lost expression in my eyes. Someone has said that the eyes are the "windows of your soul". These "windows" were misted over with the effect of so many drugs — prescribed, of course, but nevertheless eating away any spontaneity that might still be left. They were red-rimmed from crying. I despised my weakness and in so doing despised everything about myself.

Every day I would read in the paper of people so far worse off than I. People starving, people bereaved. I had wanted many times to be able to reach out and perhaps help; but always this "ME" seemed to get in the way. My life seemed so utterly useless.

One night I was having dinner with John. He was proceeding to lay the law down about my career.

"You aren't pushing yourself enough! You don't attend enough auditions! ...'

All of a sudden it seemed every fibre of my being was screaming out silently within me, "Peace! That's all I want! I have to get out of here!"

I struggled to the door of the restaurant and left him sitting at the table watching in amazement. Stumbling into the street I realised I was losing control of my legs — my mind was reeling with the sound of his voice, but I knew somehow I could catch a bus nearby that would take me to my grandmother's house.

With all the will-power I could muster I stood in the queue waiting for that bus. When it came I stumbled on and sat, not daring to even look at the other passengers. Automatically I found the fare and paid the conductor.

My hands were wet with an icy sweat and I dug my nails into the palms, fighting for control. Every nerve seemed to be on edge and the noise from the engine of the bus made the vice that seemed to be tightening around my head, excruciating.

Every noise jarred me as I fought for control.

Just to be able to get to my grandmother's house. Perhaps I could rest there and no one would know. I could keep up the act.

Then the flood gates burst forth and I cried openly in front of all the other passengers. All my desperation poured out— uncontrollably.

I could no longer hide behind the mask.

Always trying to act the perfect lady—always in control— now I felt naked as they stared.

"How disgusting, she's drunk!" I heard someone say.

I tried to defend myself, but all I could utter were sounds. I had no control over my mouth and there seemed to be coming from me a deep cry for help that could only be expressed in an agonising moan.

I had heard these sounds before, it seemed—years before —when my grandmother had tried to tell me she was ill. Being a child, I had laughed, thinking she was playing a game and had run off to school, not knowing she was asking for help.

My legs felt as if they were trapped in a quagmire and when the bus reached my stop, I dragged myself past the accusing eyes—a gibbering, uncontrollable, frightened human being.

My grandmother's house was within a few steps and I fell in the front door and let out a cry for help.

The next thing I remember was the family doctor standing by my bed saying, "The next time she has one of these hysterical outbursts, call me and I'll give her a sedative immediately."

The next time!

The only feeling that had been like a blessing to me was

that, all the floodgates having burst, there was a strange sense of relief; now I would no longer feel this terrible, stifling meaningless battle within me.

But the doctor had said, "The next time . . ."

I closed my eyes and cried silent tears, for there seemed no use in trying to battle anymore.

Why was I so weak, when others could seemingly face life's problems?

I longed to be a cabbage.

That's what I had called people who went about their everyday jobs, content to live a mundane life—catching the same train every day, doing routinely the same job and returning to the same house to eat, sleep and start the whole monotonous, dreary round again.

I did not realise that they too were wearing masks. Masks to cover their weariness which came from facing the responsibilities that loomed before them day after day.

Perhaps they envied those of us in the creative world, whose lives seemed so full of "highs" but who managed usually successfully to hide the devastating "lows".

I tried to talk but found no words came out, only sounds.

Raising my arms I tried to gesture, but my hands were contorted and would not obey me.

"Dear God, what is happening? I can no longer control my body!"

I tried to sit up and walk but could only crawl like an animal. My feet gave way underneath me, each time I would try to stand.

I began to shake in abject fear as I realised that I could no longer rely on my body to act at my every command. It was as if the home I had known for so long had been taken over by an outsider who ran rampant through the hallways of my being, flaunting everything I had tried over the years to hide and protect from the eyes of the spectators gathered to mock and shake their heads.

There are so many incidents I cannot remember regarding my breakdown because of the heavy sedation I was under. Sometimes I can remember vividly something that happened as if I had only been caught in a terrible nightmare. But unfortunately it really happened and one day I remember the doctor saying, "You will never be the same again, Joan. Your whole nervous system has been through a tremendous strain. You will always have to pace yourself. Try never to get over-tired, or you will find all the symptoms returning."

I turned my head away, not wanting to hear that I would never be the same again. I wanted to BE. To radiate vitality. To be carefree and strong. To achieve everything that was still waiting out there to be achieved. And to love and be loved—but who would want to have a burden like me in their lives?

I lay there for weeks it seemed, thinking of all my friends.

Joy Elson, with whom I had been so close at school and spent so many holidays. She had dared me to get A. E. Matthews' autograph and that had led to my becoming an actress. Now she and David Rayner were happily married with children. I felt she had achieved so much more than I.

Others I knew were married, happily, it seemed. Had I put too much of an emphasis on attaining fame at the expense of finding real happiness in marriage and children? One thing was certain now—I would never have children for I could not be trusted to be a mother.

Pace myself. Do not get over-tired. It would be laughable to say to a child, "Sorry, I'm too tired to be a mother today. Come back when I've paced myself and refuelled."

Anyway, I didn't really want children. The thought of my mother's death in childbirth terrified me. Forget the mother bit, I thought. Forget the wife bit, too. No man would want this gibbering idiot for a wife.

So what was the point of living?

To be pepped up with pep pills and to sleep with sleeping pills for the rest of my life? To have to live in this never-never land of drugs and pacing oneself was not worth the effort.

Depression followed depression.

I dreaded a new day for it held no bright hope and I dreaded the nights for they held, even with sleeping pills, either sleeplessness or terrifying nightmares.

My one dread was that everyone was talking about putting me in an asylum. Shock treatment. Locked into a room. Strait-jackets. All these visions would mock me at night and I would always sleep with the light on for fear I would be suddenly overtaken in the darkness.

My mind was playing tricks on me and it was all I could do to perform the simplest task.

Looking back it seemed as if I were forever climbing a dark mental staircase, the walls of which were gradually pressing in on me and there seemed no end to the murky, oppressive journey.

It was kept as quiet as possible that I was having "trouble". Oh, how I thank the Lord that terrible stigma is being lifted from those who suffer the indescribable torments that the mind can bring—that it is being recognised as a real illness now, and not just some imaginary condition you wish upon yourself.

Society has advanced tremendously since the days when in the 1700s and 1800s it was considered fashionable to stroll past the cages of those who were demented, as one would now stroll through a zoo. But the animals in the zoo today are treated in a far superior fashion to the luckless defenceless creatures who were chained and mocked at.

Medical science is learning more and more of the chemical

imbalances that play such an important part in the working of the brain.

The guilt that pervaded me was unbelievable.

I had let my family down—no one would ever forget that Joan Winmill had had a nervous breakdown.

I remember sometime later that I had fallen, fracturing my right hand. It had to be set and caused considerable pain. Sympathy was shown wherever I went with my hand in a cast.

"Yes, it hurts," I thought, "but if you only knew—it's nothing compared to the agonies I've been through. This hand shows, but the pain of the hidden agonies is multiplied ten thousandfold because there seems no end and no one can really understand."

My care was becoming too much for my grandmother and so I moved to my Aunt Hilda's house nearby. Their house had seen so much sorrow. First with my mother's death and then with their little son Stewart's. Now I was to burden them.

It was a tremendous task for them, but I was grateful to be there if only for a while, for Audrey was there and her bright sunny countenance always seemed to help me.

I lay awake in the bedroom of their house remembering that this was the same room where my mother had died. What had been her thoughts as she had struggled to live, I wondered? Did she ask God to help her? If she had lived, would I be locked within the depths of my own prison? Would her love and encouragement have filled the void and released this timorous being?

I thought back to my religious training and tried to pray. My words were faltering, so I stopped. The only prayers I had heard were in church and they had always been so eloquent.

But I did remember certain passages of scripture and they

would console me. A few years after my breakdown, I found a diary of mine written during that time and there, as a reminder to me of the dark days, were some of the verses from the Psalms that had comforted me. I don't remember the exact verses but they all had to do with David crying out to God and God hearing him.

One night I had a vivid dream of the crucifixion.

It was as if I were there and were actually seeing the soldiers driving the nails into Jesus's hands. I wanted to cry out to stop them, but I hung back in the crowd, afraid—not wanting to be known as one of His followers.

Then when they had finished nailing Him to the crude executionary tree, the thud of the cross being driven in the ground was horrifying. When I took my hands from my eyes, I looked up and saw, instead of Jesus on that cross, that it was me! I could not help myself, but struggled in the crowd to get to the cross and plead with soldiers to get me down.

I awakened in a pool of sweat and reached for another sleeping pill to drown out the terrifying memory.

I was so tired of not being able to swallow properly, not being able to walk or talk. If I stayed in bed much longer I would be so weak, what would happen to me?

I struggled each day to try to talk and then one day my cousin Audrey was having a one-sided conversation with me, sitting quietly embroidering. Suddenly, I found I could speak again!

To hear the sound of my own voice, normally uttering WORDS! It was unbelievable.

We laughed together and I felt so thankful that once more I had control of my tongue. (Oh, that I had had such control of my tongue in the years to follow!)

What a relief it must have been for them all, as they saw me get stronger each day. I shall always be grateful for the care they gave me, even though it was so hard on them.

Months later, I felt strong enough to return to London and after a few shaky starts, I was able to work again. But always with the fear in the back of my mind that someone would bring up the fact that I had had a breakdown and was not to be trusted in any important role, for fear I would break down again.

I had now signed with Plunket Greene, the agent, and he sent me out on many auditions. I landed a part in *The Housemaster*, the revival of a classic about a boys' school and the escapades of a professor and his, to say the least, exuberant family.

Jack Hulbert, who with his wife Cicely Courtneidge have delighted audiences on the English stage from the early 1920s in an outstanding career together, was playing the lead and directing.

I was delighted with the idea of appearing in the West End once more, for we were opening at the St Martin's Lane Theatre. My sister was to be played by Yvette Wyatt, who is a very lovely, sensitive and warm person. She was and is a real friend. During rehearsals we had many long talks about "life" — perhaps we were both still searching for something which seemed out of reach.

The days for the run of the show were ones to look forward to, and excitedly I plunged into rehearsals and fittings for clothes with the thought, "I've come full circle — nothing is going to daunt me again."

Opening night came and with it all the anticipation, nerves and exhilaration that always accompanies it.

The play was well received. Jack Hulbert was delighted with the reception and told us all how happy he was. What a rare quality he had. Talented enough to direct and star, and yet with such a human touch. He made the cast and everyone around him want to give their best. He had an

70

exuberance that was catching. I feel privileged to have worked with him.

The Housemaster was very dated, but we played it for all it was worth and the audience delighted in the rather "campy" way it was presented.

After the curtain came down and we had taken our final bow and all the effusive accolades had been distributed, I returned to the dressing room deep in thought.

"All right. What's missing? I'm back on the West End stage and this is unbelievable. Something is still missing!" My father came round to see me and was so happy that I had made it back in one piece again. So was my stepmother, Ann. Together they wished me happiness and good health from now on.

A red apple sat on my dressing room table. A token from John, who had read that is what the Barrymores sent each other on opening night. He was away on tour and could not be with me.

After the show the cast celebrated and finally it was time to go home.

I pulled out the key to my flat and opened the door with the thought, "Why am I not on top of the world? This is absolutely ridiculous. I'm back. I'm well again. I love this work. How I love it. The cast had been great. The reception was wonderful. WHY? Why? Why? There is a dimension still missing? It seems as if I am reaching for something that is unattainable. To be satisfied within oneself. To be content. To feel I belong."

I automatically reached for a sleeping pill, for I knew it would blot out all of the questions and bring the blessed oblivion once more. I wondered if being a success was worth the struggle.

Nagging inside me always was the realisation that I loved this work, even with all of its heartaches. There would always be for me a desire to immerse myself into a role and be the character that the author and director had laboured over, many times with Churchillian "blood, sweat and tears". Something in me was always wanting to "attack" a script and become the character printed there in black and white.

So it was with a great feeling of bewilderment that I began to see that my work was not enough to satisfy all that was crying out, like a starving lioness, within me.

On I went into a BBC television serialised thriller *Epitaph for a Spy* by Eric Ambler, playing the leading role opposite Peter Cushing. He is known as the star of so many horror movies that are completely opposite to his nature. He was a very gracious man and he and his wife were so helpful to me in so many ways—perhaps unaware of just how kind they were being to me, when I needed so desperately a helping hand.

I enjoyed this part greatly and felt my old confidence returning. Perhaps now I had turned the corner and I could really set out and reach my goal.

With the series came a great deal of publicity in which every actress delights. It was exciting to reach for the morning paper and see your photograph and a good story about you in black and white.

With this engagement in *Epitaph for a Spy*, I returned to all the parties and social events. It was an exciting time, mixing again with the theatre and movie "greats". Seeing Sir Noel Coward surrounded by his admirers. Partying with Sam Spiegel, Bob Hope, Zsa Zsa Gabor.

As I would look at them, always would come the thought, "Are you really happy, or is there something deep, deep down missing in your life, too?"

Everyone seemed so sure of themselves, so confident. Perhaps it was only I who expected more out of life.

I found I was now analysing every word I said and others

said to me. I would wake up in the morning remembering my conversation at a party or over dinner. Had I said the right thing? What did they mean when they had said so and so?

The mask was being fitted more securely this time. I was determined that no one should ever find out that I needed anything or anybody to make me completely happy.

I had not come to realise, like St Augustine, that our soul can never find rest, until it finds its rest in God.

One day, during a rehearsal for a further segment of *Epitaph For a Spy*, I knew again my health was cracking.

The guilt that pervaded me whispered over and over again, "You're letting your family down, you've got to keep going. Your love affair with John has to end. It's a dead end for both of you. You have to be free—free of all your mistakes."

There seemed no way out of the maze that trapped me, for I did not seem to have the strength to make a definite decision about anything.

I could not face another breakdown! With all of its heartaches and suffering. Not only for myself, but for those I loved.

The thought of suicide began to dominate my mind.

It is so strange to many that, though I had a good general knowledge of the Bible, the act of suicide did not seem to me a sin.

"Self murder," the dictionary defines suicide.

I had never thought of it in that way. Especially then. For here was a life that was not bringing happiness to myself and certainly not to others.

I had once thought seriously of doing some kind of welfare work—particularly among prisoners. I would often think as I read the reports of trials in the newspapers, "there but for the grace of God go I"—realising the need for punishment to deter crime, but imagining what it would be like to be imprisoned: to hear the door of that cell clang shut and to have to face the self-recrimination for seemingly endless days, perhaps for a crime committed on the spur of the moment.

I was a virtual prisoner—in my mind. So how could I help others. Imaginations running rampant—spurred on by the phenobarbital—depressions that brought me down to the pit of despair.

Sorry for myself? Yes.

Longing for an answer? Yes, oh yes. But where?

I walked for hours in nearby Kensington Gardens. The bleakness of winter still pervaded the park, but for a while I was free to get things in perspective as I felt the soft grass underfoot. The grey sky overhead gave vent to my feelings of wanting to be free.

In the streets of my beloved London there seemed to be endless souls all bent on finding their own solution to the pursuit of happiness. In William Blake's poem "London" he wrote:

> I wander through each chartered street,
> Near where the chartered Thames does flow
> And mark in every face I meet
> Marks of weakness, marks of woe.

Did we all have an imaginary Shangri-la that we escaped to, only to find in the morning's harsh light that it had faded and the stark reality of one's existence loomed only too frighteningly?

In all these depths of thought my father's face and my family would come before me. If I killed myself, what grief it would bring, particularly to him. He had always been so kind, always wanting to help.

I would remember the long talks we would have, sometimes parked in his car, before he would take off on a trip or when he came to meet me. These memories would check me and in my confusion would bring an island of refuge.

But it would fade as the torment grew stronger and stronger until finally I became obsessed with the thought of ending my life.

It was then in all my despair and confusion I cried out to God to help me.

So it was that at this dead-end of my life, with seemingly no answer to my most fervent needs, that the most important telephone call came. The bell ringing, ringing in my flat until finally I answered. It was an invitation to hear Billy Graham.

The caller was not even aware that God was using him to start me on life's most important and fulfilling venture.

10

I CAREFULLY SELECTED what I would wear to the Billy
Graham Crusade meeting. No one was going to think by my
outward appearance that I had a need. This was Miss Successful who had only come to be an observer and to enjoy
some friends' company. The phenobarbital would give me
courage: to meet John Mercer and his wife who had invited
me to the Crusade. I was in a vicious circle, for my nerves
were cracking and taking the barbiturate to keep me going
filled me with a hopeless depression.

But tonight I would act as if nothing was wrong with my
world. Taking a quick look in the mirror I decided I looked
successful and when I smiled, everyone would think my life
held no problems.

In four words—I was a fake.

After dinner with several friends of the Mercers, we
headed towards Haringey Arena where the Crusade was
being held. One person remarked that he couldn't wait to
see the crying converts. There had been an article in one of
the London newspapers about this and we laughed and
agreed it would be interesting.

Even as I laughed, I sensed a terrible need in my life, but
these people would never know, I assured myself.

After we were seated in the Arena, I began to look around at the people. It was incredible. It seemed like a vast cathedral. The large choir was singing "Blessed Assurance, Jesus is Mine . . ." An unfamiliar hymn to me and the words seemed almost foreign. "Blessed Assurance?" I felt none. "Jesus is mine?" Not really. He died for the sins of the *world*. He could never be said to be mine.

I looked at the people who sat on the platform. One lady stood out. She was wearing a bright red coat and an exotic yellow hat. I thought it must be Sophie Tucker. Never had I seen anyone dressed in such bright colours attending a religious service! Weeks later I was to meet that person, Miss Henrietta Mears, from the Hollywood Presbyterian Church, whose life had been used to bring so many to Christ. She was to influence my life too.

A surprise for me at the Crusade was the appearance of Dale Evans Rogers who told of her love for Jesus Christ and how He had changed her life. It was amazing to hear this well-known actress from Hollywood speaking in front of all these people—not of her achievements but of Jesus's.

In training as an actress, one has always to push oneself, but Dale told that she had realised nothing was as important in life as what you did with Christ and whether He was Lord of your life.

Then Billy Graham got up to speak. So this was the American who had come to tell the British about religion! I settled myself in my seat ready to analyse his performance and to have some witticisms for the drive home with my friends.

But God had other plans.

As I sat and listened to Dr Graham I was struck by his sincerity. Even if I did not at first agree with him, I believed he was sincere. But what was he saying about a personal

Saviour? I had been brought up in the church but had never thought about Jesus being a personal Saviour. In my belief the Jesus who had hung and suffered until death upon a cross had died for the whole world.

Then Billy said, "If you had been the only one on this earth, Jesus would have been willing to die for you: only He was pure enough to be sacrificed for your sins. God loved you so much that He sent His only Son to die for you. All *you* have to do is to realise your need, acknowledge your sin and ask Him to come into your life."

Was this oversimplifying the Bible?

I thought of what I had been taught as a child. It *was* simple the way Miss Godfrey, my Primary School Head-mistress, had taught the Scriptures and I had loved to listen to her as she had told about the teachings and life of Christ. Had I missed the significance of God's love in my quest for happiness and self satisfaction?

"For what shall it profit a man if he shall gain the whole world and lose his own soul? How many people here tonight have had no time for God because of their ambition for material things?"

Wow! That was a blow right between the eyes. He was getting personal now.

For me, knowledge of Jesus Christ had been enough. When I left school I remember thinking, "I've got to get on in this world and if people know that I believe in God, maybe it will stop me getting on in some circles—so I will keep it to myself." How selfish. I had wanted to take all of God's blessings, but I had been ashamed of His Son and in that moment, as Billy Graham spoke, I realised that I was indeed a sinner who needed Jesus so much.

"Seek ye first the kingdom of God and His righteousness and all these things shall be added unto you," Billy Graham quoted from Matthew 6 : 33.

"Oh, God, I have not put You first in my life. It has all been self-seeking."

I had laughed at the words "saved" and "sinner". Now here I was confronted with Christ. Not the One whom I had seen hanging on a cross in a beautiful Rennaissance painting —but a living Redeemer.

"There are many who believe suicide to be the answer to their problems!"

Had John Mercer told Billy Graham about me? He worked for Lloyd's of London, who were insuring the Crusade, but surely John did not know my secret thoughts of the past weeks. Did they show in my face? I glanced quickly at John, but there didn't seem to be any clue by his expression.

"You cannot run away from your problems. But by coming to the foot of the cross and realising your need of forgiveness, you can find peace that passes all understanding through accepting Christ."

Peace. How I had longed for peace and looked for it in so many ways. Always wanting to find the answer to life, wanting to belong. Needing to be understood. What a terrible mess I had made of this life that God had given to me. I had even thought about ending it, "Lord. Forgive me. But I don't have the courage to face it any more alone. I want to give my life to you, but I'm so terribly afraid of what these friends will think. Dear God, give me the courage to turn this life over to you."

I sat there praying and watching the crowds go towards the platform to give their lives to Christ. And there I sat. Held back by my thoughts of being laughed at by my friends. But I continued to pray and then it seemed I realised that important as it was what my friends thought of me, it was far more important what God thought of me. Suddenly, I felt myself stand—God had given me the courage to make this decision—and I stepped out into the aisle.

Dale Evans' voice came back to me as I remembered her telling of what Christ meant to her and I thought, "For the first time in my life, I'm not ashamed to let others know I believe in Jesus Christ."

11

You started on the Great Quest the moment
you were born . . . Searching for something you
never had . . . At the loneliest moments in your
life, you have looked at other men and women
and wondered if they too were seeking—
seeking something they couldn't describe, but
knew they wanted and needed.

> Billy Graham

It is hard to conceive that by a childlike response to an
invitation to "accept" Christ as Saviour, there could be such
a drastic change in my life.

Yet this is exactly what happened.

That night at Haringey Arena, as I stood by the platform
along with so many others, I had finally reached a decision.
I was no longer tossed in my mind as to what the future held.
I had reached a point of no return, for this transaction was
with God.

Simply—I had given everything over to Christ. All my
heartaches, longings, ambitions. Uppermost in my mind was
the realisation that everything had been self-seeking in my
life. Now instead of always comparing myself with others,
my yardstick of perfection was Jesus.

His selfless life made mine utterly contemptible. But I was also tremendously aware of the magnitude of His love.

There was now a light at the end of the tunnel.

I had felt compelled to answer an invitation that Billy Graham had given—me, who had always calculatingly tried to hide any feelings of need from my friends. Now I was standing before an audience of 12,000 people attesting to the fact that I did need Someone.

My mind was blurred from the drugs, but there were very vivid thoughts that whirled at breakneck speed through my befuddled brain.

"My friends—what can I say to them?"

"Maybe I can slip away and no one will notice me."

The crowd that had come forward was now being escorted out of the Arena to a destination unknown.

We passed through nondescript halls until we were ushered into a large room. I could see that people were beginning to sit and talk and that was the last thing I wanted to do. I did not want to discuss what I had done with anyone, so I gradually edged my way to the back of the room making a slow bee-line for the exit.

"No one will notice," I thought.

But alas, I was spotted, for out of the corner of my eye I saw a lady approaching me, complete with Bible.

"Trapped," I mused. "I don't want to talk to anyone." A fear enveloped me—again not wanting people to know of my need.

Perhaps you have had the joy of meeting someone only for a few moments and you feel as if they care and understand. As I turned in acknowledgment of her greeting, I sensed that here was a person who did indeed care.

Her face had an openness of expression and I can only say that my first thoughts were "What a truly beautiful woman! She has such an aura of serenity. How I long for this."

Her dark hair was styled in a "page boy" which was offset by a camel-coloured coat. Simply, but elegantly dressed.

She talked to me for a while, but my mind was racing again.

"I must not let her know how I really feel ..."

She read from the Bible and prayed with me, but all I could remember from our conversation was, "Don't forget, Joan, you don't walk out of here alone—Christ goes with you!"

The reassurance of these words lived with me and I was to find they were inexplicably true. But at that moment I merely could cling to them like a child—afraid that someone or something would take it away.

The lady in the camel-coloured coat was talking to me again.

"Would you like to meet my husband?"

I nodded assent and followed her back through the halls from where most of the crowds had dispersed.

I wondered why she wanted me to meet her husband. My mind was beginning to play tricks on me and I didn't trust my speech. The phenobarbital was wearing off and I did not want to stutter.

We arrived at an unmarked door and after knocking, she opened it to reveal a small dressing room. To my surprise the occupant was Billy Graham!

They ushered me in and I was asked to sit down. Apart from the fact that I was not sure if my speech would betray me, the shock of the husband turning out to be Billy Graham had me completely dazed.

He was so enthusiastic and proceeded to say how delighted he was about my decision—Ruth, his wife, explaining what had happened.

I was so overwhelmed that all I could say in reply to his questions was an occasional, "Yes—no—yes—no."

It was several years later Ruth told me Billy had asked her that night, "Do you really think we got through to that girl?"

I met my group of friends and we drove home. I do not remember a word being spoken and if there was I was oblivious to any conversation.

Thanking them, I got out of the car and opened the door of the large Edwardian house that held my flat. My thoughts were manifold as I walked through the familiar rooms.

Something had happened in my life. Ruth Graham had said I was no longer alone—Christ was with me.

I hunted for the dark red Bible my father had given me so many years ago and began to read—as if for the first time.

Familiar passages were read over and over.

"Behold I am with you . . ."

"Blessed are the poor in spirit . . ."

"For God so loved the world . . ."

Sitting in the same armchair that had been the scene of many hopeless depressions, I felt His presence with me and rejoiced that no longer was my life filled with despair.

First of all, I decided, with God's help I was going to change many situations.

I would move from here, with all of its lonely, unhappy memories.

I would once and for all end the relationship with John French that was only tearing both of us apart.

With these resolutions made I fell asleep that night with my mind full of questions, but for the first time in years—hope.

The next morning dawned, a typical London late March hazy, cold morning. But my first thoughts were of Christ. I knew He was with me! I determined to begin looking for a new flat in which to start my new life. The day was spent viewing prospective new homes until I finally settled on one in Kensington, near to the Royal Albert Hall and only a few minutes' walk from the Kensington Gardens I loved.

I was worn out that night when I returned to face the flat but there was a feeling of accomplishment. The inevitable packing began as I could not wait to get out of the depressing atmosphere. I had tried that day not to take any phenobarbital, but my body was so used to it; by bedtime it seemed every nerve was jumping. I reached for a sleeping pill to dull my senses and sank into the never-never land I had become accustomed to.

Now came the decision to tell John it was definitely all over. I struggled desperately to tell him it was finished, but no courage seemed to come.

What had I done? There had been no real change in my life!

A simple act of walking forward to stand at a platform could not transform me. "Perhaps momentarily—but I am still the same."

I suddenly began to cry as the hopelessness of my life started to crowd in again. But even then I found myself praying.

"Dear Lord, if You really care, help me now! I'm sinking back again. Maybe it was a mistake planning to move from here and then to face the devastating upset of finishing past relationships."

Reaching into my handbag for a Kleenex, I came across a small packet of Bible verses Ruth Graham had given me that night. I had thought, "Fine for somebody else, but not for me" and had promptly forgotten them. But now I found myself looking at them.

Ruth had said, "Memorise these, Joan, they will help you grow stronger in Christ."

I looked at them hoping for some kind of strength, when I came to I Corinthians 10.13:

There hath no temptation taken you, but such as is
common to man: but God is faithful, who will not
suffer you to be tempted above that ye are able;
but will with the temptation make a way to escape,
that ye may be able to bear it.

"Oh God—You've promised—You've promised! You
said You'd be faithful and not let me be tempted more than
I can bear. Please help me now. I want to slide back— it's
easier, Lord."

In the unhappiness there was a feeling of just being able
to sink into oblivion. "Now I don't seem to have the strength
again to change my life. God, I believe You will make a way
to escape, only right now I am sinking—wanting to take the
easy way out."

I began to memorise the verse as I packed. I, who would
have laughed at the idea a few days ago, now was asking
God to help me resist the temptation of taking the easy way
out. It was so hard.

Moving day came and I made myself keep going—my cat
Willie inspected his new headquarters and seemed to find
them acceptable.

Once moved in I felt a tremendous sense of joy come over
me and I danced—the only expression that came naturally
to me at that moment. David had danced before the Lord: I
danced from room to room of my new home, praising Him
and thanking Him for the release that had flooded through
me.

I passed Hyde Park Corner that day. The daffodils had
never before looked so beautiful to me. Someone had said,
"From now on you will never look at the world in quite the
same way," and it was true.

I began to find I could put my life in perspective. Always
before my thinking had been coloured by what "I" wanted

to achieve. My horizons had been boxed in and there was no room for eternal values.

Eternity loomed before me. Life was to be lived each day with that in mind. But it was not a subject to be dreaded —as I read Jesus's promises in the Bible of the joy that awaited us with Him.

One day, however, after having unsuccessfully auditioned for a play, I came back to my new flat tired and feeling depressed. I was still on a see-saw as far as my emotions were concerned.

Opening the front door, I noticed a small parcel lying on the mat addressed to me. Tearing the wrapper off, I found inside a book entitled *Peace With God* by Billy Graham, and in it a note from Ruth hoping I would enjoy it and asking me to call her and have tea.

I was deeply impressed that she had taken the time to send the book to me. Her note cheered me and made me realise again that here was a person who really cared. God used her again in my life, just when I needed a touch of His love.

I went to bed early that night and began to read *Peace With God*.

In the early morning I awakened—the book still open and two-thirds read. There were so many answers to questions I had had for so long as to *why* I was here. Suddenly the finiteness of my life took new meaning. This body that I moved around in is going to die one day, but the real me, the me that loves, feels deep longings that cannot be put into words—that me will live on. By Christ's sacrifice on the cross, I will be deemed worthy to enter heaven and *only* through Christ for there is nothing we can achieve on this earth that can make us worthy. But the joy of knowing this seemed to flood through me as I thought of all there was to look forward to.

I hastily picked up the phone and dialled a familiar number. A friend with whom I had been in a TV series. A very platonic friendship had developed and it was always good to be with him, because he made me laugh. Now as I told him what had happened in my life—I made him laugh. Finally, laughing so hard, he told me he would have to call me back after he got control of himself.

I put the telephone down and felt that I was an absolute failure as a Christian. The old me was hurt. I hated the thought of being laughed at and criticised. It was so much easier to go with the crowd.

Looking at *Peace With God*, I remembered the note that Ruth had put inside it inviting me to tea. I dialled the number of the hotel and asked for her room number. Imagine my confusion when Billy Graham answered. Again he was so enthusiastic and delighted about my decision for Christ. Again all I could say was "Yes—no—yes—no!"

Ruth came on the phone and we made arrangements to have tea at the hotel the next day. I looked forward to seeing her again.

Next day found me at the hotel a little early for my appointment, so I decided to just wait in the lobby unobtrusively watching people come and go. A marvellous field for an actress to watch the mannerisms of the unsuspecting guests as they made their exits and entrances.

Little did I know that I was the object of observation. A young attractive girl approached me and said, "Hi. I'm Leila . . . Aren't you Joan Winmill? Why, I have really been praying for you!"

This just shook me to the core. To think that this girl, whom I had never met would be praying for ME. I was deeply touched and thanked her. She explained that she was working with the Billy Graham Team as a Counsellor with the women, and was loving her stay in London. I immediately felt from her the same warmth and genuine concern that Ruth had exuded when I met her. To see this young, attractive American girl talking so naturally about praying for someone, completely without embarrassment, and expressing her faith in Christ was quite a revelation to this High Anglican who found it difficult to express her faith to anyone. (Even more so after my experience on the telephone with my friend the day before.) Meeting Leila was to be an experience I would never forget and over the years her friendship meant so much to me. Later, when we were both married, we had yet another bond in Christ for our first-born sons arrived on the same day and we often celebrated their mutual birthdays.

Leila is now with her Lord. She died from cancer, leaving a beautiful family. I can remember when her husband, Doug Sparks, had to go on so many journeys as his work with the Navigators kept him travelling constantly. Leila confided to me one day how she would long for his return. Now she has gone ahead of him, unafraid because she knew her destination.

Tea that afternoon with Ruth was a time of listening to a person who was so in contact with Christ. I had never met people like this before who could talk so naturally about Him. He seemed to fill her whole life.

Ruth and I prayed together and I sensed even though there was still so much to be changed in my life, that He was listening and would continue to guide me. Then Ruth gave me a red leather Bible, inscribed from her and Billy.

To Joan Winmill — God bless you. Billy Graham
"Being confident of this very thing, that He which hath begun a good work in you, will perform it until the day of Jesus Christ." Phil 1 : 6.
We love you Joan, and will be holding you up in our prayers. Ruth Graham

"Now unto Him that is able to keep you from
falling and to present you faultless before
the presence of His glory with exceeding joy."
Jude 24.

I was deeply touched and could not find words to express
all that I felt. The gift of *Peace With God* had moved me
deeply and now this, too. I thanked her and wished that my
English reticence could be swept aside to tell all that was in
my heart.

Years later Ruth told me that the day before I came to
tea, she had felt she should go home, as she said she really
wasn't being too much help to anyone. Billy was so busy
with the Crusade and she kept thinking of her children back
in Montreat, North Carolina, and felt so homesick for them.
Then I called and arranged to have tea with her and she
received a letter from another girl whom she was able to
help. It so often seems to happen in our lives that just when
we feel we are not needed the Lord says, "Wait, I have a few
lambs who need you. Love them through me."

Ruth's love and understanding could never begin to be
equated that day, but I do know that He had her there in my
life when I so desperately needed the love of a fellow Christian who had walked many more miles with Him and knew
He did not let you down, no matter what the circumstances.

I left the hotel feeling stronger and taller as I returned to
my new flat, with the new red Bible under my arm just burning to be read. Which is exactly what I did do as soon as I
reached home. The print was readable, not like the usual
Bible I had been used to and I read avidly for hours, under-
lining verses that seemed to leap out at me, demanding my
attention.

There was the question of going back to church again now
and I decided I would put that off for a long time. I did not

want personalities or theology to spoil this new found personal experience I had found with Christ. Ruth sensed this and encouraged me to find a church I could be happy in.

I'll never forget what happened to me one Sunday morning in April. I awakened and had the tremendous urge to want to go to church — it was the Holy Spirit working in me, giving me the desire. I did not have to force myself to go — I wanted to go and worship Him!

"I was glad when they said unto me, let us go into the house of the Lord!" Psalm 122.

Oh, David had put into words what was in my heart as I walked down the Brompton Road, past Harrods, to the beautiful church of St Margaret's.

When I walked in the choir was singing a glorious anthem, praising God, and the whole church resounded to the voices and to the magnificent organ. I felt transported out of my everyday feelings into a closer relationship of worship with Christ.

The Creed took on new meaning.

"I believe in God the Father Almighty and in His Son, Jesus Christ our Lord."

He was my Lord now. I had given this life over to Him and now I sat in the beauty of this majestic edifice that had been built to glorify God, like a small child who had suddenly been given all that her heart desired. To be loved like this, by God who had cared enough to send His Son to die for my sins was at once exalting and humbling at the same time. I felt so unworthy and yet bathed in a love that could only come from God.

My flat would now be the scene of a weekly Bible study, for the Crusade organisers had gathered together some of the names of those who had made decisions and were anxious to learn more of this new found life in Christ. We started with eight and the numbers grew so quickly; I knew why the Lord had provided me with a large living room. I eagerly awaited Thursday evenings as we discussed what had happened to us during the week—the blessings and the stumblings. Then Rev. Bruce Reed would arrive and teach us from the Bible more of the exciting promises we could find there. My Bible became dog-eared and worn as I marked it and studied each day, this once-dry book that now came alive each time I picked it up and read the beautiful literature that had been waiting for so long to be read by me. Far from dead, it was alive to today's problems.

I still have the Bible Billy and Ruth gave me and I treasure each worn, patched page. I have read and reread over and over again this Love Story from God.

John and I were growing further and further apart, and I longed for him to be able to find this joy I now had; but he could not stand to have me talk about Christ. Especially since finding Him, I had changed so much and was no longer clinging to John simply out of the fear of being lonely.

I prayed so much that John would come to know Christ and perhaps in his finding Him we could have a life together. But it was not to be as far as a life together was concerned, for God had other plans for both of us. Sometimes there has to come a parting in our lives to make us completely dependent on God. Friends did not understand. They thought I considered myself too good for him. John did not understand and even now it is difficult to put down in words all that happened. But I continued to pray that God would work out this heartbreaking problem.

12

ONE MORNING EARLY, the telephone rang and it was Len Reeves, the producer of the commercial I had done for Silvikrin shampoo. He was asking me to read for a part in a film he was working on for Billy Graham. I was really floored and rushed around wondering just what I would wear. The telephone rang again. This time it was my agent saying he wanted me to go in an hour and audition for the part of a prostitute. I really wondered how I should dress now! I would not have time to get home to change before having to meet the director of the Billy Graham film, and the roles were obviously going to be poles apart. I decided to rely on lots of jewellery for the prostitute part, and to discard most of it for the spiritual part!

I read for the prostitute and did not feel as if I had gone over too well. Maybe I needed more than jewellery to get me the part. Then I rushed over to the hotel to audition for Billy Graham's director, Dick Ross.

Looking back, I am amazed they could even have the faith to listen to me for I had a very bad attack of sinus and could only talk as if I had adenoids. I kept assuring them I did not usually speak like this. When I started reading the script, I saw so much of my own life in it that I wondered if they had been spying on me!

Apparently, they had cast most of the film but could not find the right girl to play the lead part of an actress who after much searching and heartache comes to know Christ through a Billy Graham Crusade!

Later I learned that when Dick Ross was talking to Ruth Graham about the role, she had said, "Why, I counselled an actress the other night. Wouldn't it be interesting to have someone who had actually been converted to Christ through Bill's meetings play the role?"

When Dick Ross told me I had the part, my first feeling was of complete unworthiness because there was so much still wrong in my life. But I was assured that they wanted me to play Ann Woodbridge in *Souls in Conflict*. It was to be the start of a wonderful association with Dick Ross and later his wife, Wanda.

The atmosphere, under Dick Ross' direction, was something I had never known before. We would start each day with prayer on the set. "What a wonderful idea," I thought —until he called on me to lead in prayer one morning. I just wanted to be swallowed up by the floor. I had never prayed in public before and here I was in front of many people who didn't even believe the way I did—so many of the technicians, etc. Somehow I falteringly prayed for a blessing for the day and the Lord's guidance on the film. It was a traumatic experience for me, but one that later on I was glad I had gone through. Gradually as I became more aware of God's love to me it became a more natural thing to pray to Him in public. I would remember how much my own father loved me and how he loved to converse and hear from me.

Also appearing in the film was a very beautiful American actress Colleen Townsend, who had married Louis Evans, Junior. "Coke" had been a starlet in Hollywood. When Christ came into her life she decided a film career was not for her. She married Louis and together they were living in

Scotland, while he studied for his divinity degree.

Working with her was a heartwarming experience. She helped this bewildered new Christian in so many ways by her gentleness of spirit and completely natural attitude towards others. I watched her life very closely.

Ruth Graham said, "I don't think there is a mean bone in her body!"

And it was true! Arriving at the studio with her at five-thirty in the morning, I only later found she was expecting a baby yet she was always loving and uncomplaining. Coke has since written *A New Joy* and *Love is an Everyday Thing* — both titles she completely radiates in her own life.

After finishing the shooting of the film it was time for all the Billy Graham team, Dick Ross and Coke to go back to America and I missed them all. I felt as if I had known them all my life and there was still so much to learn of this new Christian road that I was now journeying on, falling so many times and wanting to say, "I'll never make it. The Lord is going to get so tired of me making so many stupid mistakes!"

The Thursday evening Bible classes kept me going from week to week. "Bible classes", just the words made me want to laugh when I thought of how opposed I had always been to anything organised as far as religion was concerned. Now I was actually having Christians meet in my flat.

There did not seem too much work going around in the theatre at this time, or so it seemed. I was offered the leading role in *The Little Hut* which would be touring England. I jumped at the part without reading the script, as it would be good publicity for me.

I shall never forget one Thursday night when the Bible class was going on I made my apologies and told everyone I would not be able to be with them as I had to read through the script for the following day. I sat in the next room looking over my part for the first time. The script was new and crisp and just the feel of it in my hands made me excited.

As I read it I suddenly realised it would be considered risqué by many Christians, to say the least. (Though by today's standards it would probably pass as family entertainment.) It was the story of three people shipwrecked on an island—a wife, her husband and her lover. I could just imagine all the criticism that would come my way, as by now I had received a great deal of publicity in the newspapers concerning my conversion. Then it hit me! What really counted was what it would do to my relationship with the Lord. Would *He* condemn my being in the play? Would it be a hindrance to others finding Him?

I decided that the next day I would ask them to release me from my contract. The answer was no. The publicity for the show was already out and that was that. I can only tell you that I learned my lines, gave no thought to them, delivered a long monologue seated on a tree trunk looking out into the audience completely blank and got the best reviews I have ever received. It was ironic.

I also got some pretty hot fan mail too, from Christians.

This made me feel unbelievably low and I read my Bible in the dressing room and asked the Lord for His guidance. His—not people's.

I waited and nothing seemed to happen in response to that prayer. The play went on touring until we reached Cardiff.

On Saturday evening, just after the curtain came down for the final show in that city, I was in my dressing room taking off my make-up when there came a knock on the door. Calling out, "Come in!" I turned and there stood a tousled haired young man, in a tousled suit grinning from ear to ear.

"What a story! 'Billy Graham Convert in Lewd Play!' How do you do. I'm a reporter with the local newspaper here."

My heart sank as I asked him to sit down.

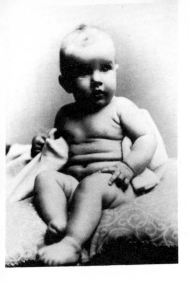

My first appearance
before a camera!

One of the world's most
gentle men — my Father

The last photo of my dear Mother

Nanny poses in her
fancy dress costume

In *The Harassed Hero* with Gabrielle Brune

"Just Married"

From *Souls in Conflict* with Colleen Townsend Evans

Speaking in a London church

Aboard the *Queen Elizabeth I*
returning to America, 1968

Billy Graham and I watch as Tricia Nixon Cox greets Ethel Waters on the occasion of her 60 years in show business

On our front doorstep in Sherman Oaks, California

David doing a "wheelie" for Bill and me outside our
California home

On the set of *Time To Run*, director Jimmy Collier discusses a scene with me

Arriving at the Hollywood premiere of *Time To Run* with Ruth Graham

Taken in our living room with "Bruno", a friend's
Yorkshire terrier

"Lord, You've got to give me the right words to say." The silent prayer went up as I sat smiling at this young man, sizing him up, while he did the same with me.

"I'd much rather you didn't, you know. I really don't need that kind of publicity right now."

"But I can't pass up a story like this," he said. "It will be great!"

There was only one thing to do and I did it. I poured out my heart to this young man, telling him all that the Lord had done in my life. That as a new Christian I was still floundering and perhaps it had been wrong to take this part; but I still had so much to learn.

He listened, then said, "It's all very interesting, but I do have a job to do."

"All right," I said, "I'll give you an interview if you promise me one thing."

"That's a deal," he said.

"Come with me to church tomorrow morning." He looked completely flabbergasted for a moment and then smilingly agreed.

We met the next day and went to a beautiful old church for the eleven o'clock service. The service was long, but inspiring, and the Welsh voices had me completely transported.

As we came out of the church into the bright sunlight he turned, shook me by the hand, and said, "You can forget about the story."

During the service God had spoken to him in the quietness of his heart and I whispered a silent, "Thank you, Lord."

Through this experience I learned two things. First, when you make a mistake God does hear and helps you if the cry comes from a contrite heart. Secondly, if I were to be a follower of His, I was going to have to be more discerning in the parts that I took from now on.

"But Lord, I may starve. So please help me. Do You want

me to give up my career and go into Christian work? I feel so confused. But again You have promised to take care of me and I thank You for that."

I had read in the New Testament that He had promised in Matthew 6:31:

Therefore take no thought, saying What shall we eat? or, What shall we drink? or, Wherewithal shall we be clothed? For after all these things do the Gentiles seek: for your heavenly Father knoweth that ye have need of all these things. But seek ye first the kingdom of God and His righteousness; and all these things shall be added unto you.

How lovingly He was telling me to trust Him. I could be exhorted by some Christians (sometimes I thought they felt they were called to "The Grand Calling of Exhorters" and nothing else), always giving unasked-for advice when at this stage in my Christian life I needed love and understanding and being pointed over and over again to His Word. But— lovingly.

Ruth Graham, each time I had asked her for advice would say, "Why don't you ask the Lord to show you what you should do? Read the Bible and ask Him to enlighten you through His Word."

This would make me want to read the Bible more and more, instead of it being a dreaded book.

Each time I did this a verse I had read would keep "nagging" me all day and I would know that it was God's way of talking to me about my problem.

"Seek ye first the kingdom of God . . ."

Was I seeking God's will for my life, or was I still holding on to both worlds. I searched my heart, not knowing if I *was* completely in His will.

Arriving back in London after the finish of the tour, I collapsed in my flat trying to sort everything out. Then came the invitation to go to America for personal appearances with *Souls in Conflict* — I was dumbfounded! It would mean travelling all over America, speaking before thousands of people. Speaking! This terrified me. Before I had always appeared behind the cover of another character, shielded by the author's words, not mine. I accepted, in fear and trembling, and began to pack for the new adventure.

This surely was an answer to my prayer concerning my future. It was the next step He wanted me to take and I could never have taken it without Him.

I bought the *Evening News* and there on the front page was a story about my appearance in New York the following week. It was then as I read it I found out that my first appearance would be in Carnegie Hall, of all places! I had read so often of the great artists who had appeared in concert there and now here was I scheduled to speak. I felt so inadequate.

As I packed I prayed that the Lord would guide this bewildered, ill-prepared child of His for all that lay ahead.

My father and Ann came to the airport to see me off and John was there too. He looked dejected and said he felt as if I had completely deserted him now for all the excitement that was waiting for me in the USA. I felt terrible as I boarded the plane, wondering if I were doing the right thing. But it seemed as though I had been swept up out of all my wonderings and questionings and literally flown out to be able to sort things out objectively. I felt sad knowing that John could not understand all that had happened in my life. Perhaps this time would be used to let the Lord speak to him — I did not know, I could only hope.

13

As the skyline of New York came into view I looked down at those famous buildings looming below. They seemed like huge silent sentinels waiting to greet me. The plane landed and as the doors opened I could not believe the gust of hot air that blew into the passenger area. It was 96 degrees and the humidity was 100 per cent. Here I was dressed for winter in the same red coat I had worn to hear Billy Graham at Haringey, a black wool suit and, to top it off, a Garboesque white felt hat. Walking down the steps I looked as out of place as a bikini in an igloo! It was Indian summer! I thought of all the clothes I had brought with me and groaned—nothing at all suitable for this heat.

Everything looked so different from London. The cars, the people, the buildings. I really felt a foreigner even though I spoke the same language. In the distance I could see some people waiting at the barrier. I thought one was Cliff Barrows, Billy Graham's songleader. Getting closer, I realised it was not he but someone that could easily be mistaken for his brother. He put out his hand and said, "Hi! I'm Bill Brown—welcome to America!"

There was something in that greeting that made me take a long look at this handsome, virile American. Bill was working for the Billy Graham Film Ministry and was in charge of the premières on the East Coast. With him was Walter Smyth, his boss, and together they took me to my hotel overlooking Central Park. We lunched, during which time Dr Smyth briefed me on my schedule while in New York. The world première was the following night at Carnegie Hall and my stomach churned at the thought of it. The Lord would really have to give me the words to say as I felt so totally inadequate. The thought of the vast size of Carnegie Hall filled me with terror.

After lunch they decided to whisk me off to Madison Square Garden to a rodeo. Sitting there boiling from the heat, I began to boil with indignation at the treatment of the animals.

"My, they would never allow this in England," I kept remarking. "It is so cruel the way they throw the animals around!"

Bill Brown, who was sitting next to me kept glancing my way.

"What a dumb blonde," his looks implied. Little did I know that before coming to the airport to meet me, someone had asked where he was going.

"Oh, out to the airport to meet some dumb blonde actress from England!"

The source insists that is exactly what he said—he still denies it.

I wonder!

The reason they had taken me to the rodeo was because Roy and Dale Rogers were starring in it and they thought it would be enjoyable for me to meet them—Dale having been such an influence on me at the Crusade. I was delighted to meet her, even though I was in a shocked, overheated state.

Next day we made our way over to Carnegie Hall for the première of the film. I sat on the platform and thought of all the great artistes who had performed there—which did not help my feeling of inadequacy one bit. In fact, it made me feel even more insignificant.

"Please, Lord, just help me to say the right thing. I don't want to let you down."

When it came my turn to speak I wondered if I could ever make it to the podium. I simply tried to tell the audience what the film had meant to me during the making of it. I also told of how the Lord had helped me through some extremely difficult days. It was His love and grace that had given me the strength I needed and in giving my life to Him I had accepted the gift of eternal life through Jesus Christ. I felt unworthy, yet He had forgiven and forgotten the past.

I sat down and hoped no one could see my knees shaking. Then the lights went down and the film was presented. I could not imagine how people would respond to Christ through a motion picture and was amazed as I watched the reaction it had. Invited to accept Him at the end of the film, scores got up and came forward just as I had at the Crusade. It was the same message, only on film and God used His word to reach these people.

I was elated and overjoyed to think the film had met with this kind of response. Everyone I spoke with afterwards was delighted and I was sailing on cloud nine—until . . . A little old lady came up to me shaking her fist in my face.

"Go back to England where you belong!" she said. "You've only come over here for the money—just like the English!"

If only she knew at that moment I would willingly have left on the next plane out, for another lady was also waiting to pounce on me.

"Don't cross your legs when you are on the platform. Looks disgusting!"

I reeled as I listened to the two of them tear me apart,

thanked them with a plastic smile and returned to Bill and company a little amazed by the heated criticism.

Afterwards, back at the hotel, there was a reception and Bill Brown's family (or rather, part of it) was there. They were a bubbly lot—so full of enthusiasm and a zest for living. I wondered what vitamins they took because I would love to have half their energy!

The days ahead were exciting ones. I travelled all over the States and everywhere I was met at the airport with a large entourage, whisked into a car, and taken through the city. Whereupon I was shown all the sights, taken to a hotel where I rested, and then appeared on TV and radio plus being interviewed by the Press. Then came the film showings at night.

In Nashville, I almost died of embarrassment. At the airport to greet me was Pek Gunn (a dedicated layman) and his wife, Frances, complete with a large contingent of police cars. I had never been in a police car before and felt like a criminal as I raced through town with sirens screaming all the way to the Governor's for tea.

Driving up to the huge southern mansion I saw many cars and realised I would not be the only one there. It was like a scene from *Gone With the Wind*, with the stately white house and its majestic columns rising up from the beautiful grounds around it.

Inside a reception was being held for me. I felt honoured as I had simply thought I was to be the only guest of Governor Frank Clements and his wife for tea. After many introductions I was handed a plate and a cup. I looked around for the saucer and out of the corner of my eye discovered everyone had their cup on the plate. Sensible, but never done in England. There, we balanced our cups and saucers until the spoon rattled and usually fell off while in the other hand we juggled with the plate and its contents.

My travelling companion was Irene Johnson, who had spent many hours with me in London, studying the Bible, answering my questions. I shall always be grateful to her for the patience she showed a very dizzy actress who had so much to learn about His grace. Irene was able to appreciate exactly what seemed to be troubling me. When the crowds of people had really affected me, she was able to help me relax with her great sense of humour and bring me down to earth again.

Upon my arrival in Houston, Texas, I met the Carlos Morris family. Carlos had just suffered a heart attack and was mending slowly. His wife, Doris, took me in to meet this man who had been felled by the illness that suddenly strikes so many active people. In spite of all he had suffered, he was optimistic and thanking the Lord for His goodness.

His mother asked if the following afternoon she could show me some of Houston's interesting sights. It had been kept for leisure time so I accepted willingly. I was instantly drawn to this delightful lady.

After we had visited some of the usual tourist stops she turned to me and said, "Joan, there's someone I want you to meet who will be able to help you in the future."

She leaned forward and instructed her chauffeur to take us to a certain address. Looking out of the window of the car, I noticed we were gradually leaving the affluent part of town and entering the poorer section. The car stopped outside a little wooden house.

"This is where the person lives who is supposed to help me?" I wondered.

It proved to be the highlight of my stay in Houston, for living in that little house was a lady who had been bedridden for many years, but who had a radiance about her I will always remember. No one entering her bedroom could help but sense that here was someone who knew the comfort of the living Christ. Mrs Morris and I prayed with her and talked with her very briefly. I needed to meet that lady, as the accolades and attention I was receiving had begun to go to my head.

On our way back to the hotel, Mrs Morris said to me, "Joan, it's easy to serve Him when everything is going just right. But the true test comes when you are alone with Him day after day on a bed of pain. Or just simply facing life's everyday problems."

I have remembered her words so many times, as the years that lay ahead brought their share of problems, for I found the same Christ who sustained that little lady in her confined room was there to help me too.

My next stop would be Hollywood. I could hardly wait to see this Golden City with all the glamour it held.

The Bill Beales met me at the airport. Bill was working with the film ministry on the west coast. He and his wife Elvera are warm delightful people. Instantly I knew that this was a couple with whom I could really feel at home. They understood the pressure I was under and shielded me from some of the "flak" that was now to break around me.

John had gone to the Press in England and said I was a modern day Joan of Arc being sacrificed at the stake for the sake of the Billy Graham Organisation. It made all the London papers and I panicked inside. The phone began to ring in my room. Reporters from *Newsweek*, *The New York Times* and other papers all over the country were now asking for interviews.

That night Dick and Wanda Ross invited me to Lawrys Restaurant to introduce me to a real American roast beef dinner. We were going to relax after quite a day. Now we could just enjoy the succulent roast beef and the beautiful surroundings. But no, the waiter approached me and said I was wanted on the telephone. At the hotel, I had foolishly left word where I could be reached. I excused myself and went to the phone. It was a long distance call from New York. The *Daily Express* and its New York correspondent were demanding an explanation of why I had been sacrificed "at the stake" à la Joan of Arc. I told him I had not been coerced into anything, but was here of my own free will. He still wanted to see me and would be flying out to Hollywood the next day.

I staggered back to the table, apologising for the interruption, and began to tuck into the glorious food when I was summoned once more to the phone. More reporters called all evening and I never think of Lawrys Prime Rib Restaurant without thinking of what happened while eating that night.

Newspapers across America carried major stories and even *Newsweek* had a photo of me complete with the incredible news item of my "sacrifice". Reporters were invited to the house of Lionel Mayell in Altadena, where I was scheduled to speak the next night. If you can imagine speaking when a "bolshi" *Daily Express* reporter is sitting on the front row, you can glimpse a little of what I suffered that night!

Before opening my mouth I said, silently, "Lord, give me the words. You can do it. I am just going to be depending on that verse in Philippians, "I can do all things through Christ, which strengtheneth me.""

At the close of my testimony and talk, the *Daily Express* gentleman shook me by the hand and said, "You don't have to worry. The story will be a kind one."

The others said similar things. I can only say I thanked the Lord again that night for His love and protection. In Jeremiah, it says:

Do not be afraid of their faces: for I am with
thee to deliver thee, saith the Lord. Then the Lord

put forth His hand and touched my mouth. And the Lord said unto me, Behold I have put my words in your mouth." Jeremiah 1 : 8, 9.

These were the verses I had clung to as I had spoken to so many thousands of people across America and those words had not failed me as I spoke face to face with those who had come to judge in a living room in the Los Angeles suburbs.

Perhaps the highlight of my stay in Hollywood, which far outdid the première of the film, was visiting the home of Henrietta Mears, the lady dressed in such bright colours whom I had seen on the platform at the Haringey Crusade. She welcomed me to her magnificent Bel Air home, but it was not the lovely surroundings that had me in awe. It was her quiet, gentle, loving way of talking to me about Jesus.

As we sat and talked, I told her how worried I was as to what the Lord would have me do with my life. Whether to stay on in the theatre and be a witness for Him there like Dale Evans, or whether to take up full-time work for Him.

"First of all, a child of God should never be worried. Concerned maybe, but never worried, because He has your life completely in His hands and He is going to show you just what He wants you to do."

We prayed together and then she opened her Bible and read me these words, "Commit thy way unto the Lord; trust also in Him; and He shall bring it to pass." Psalm 37 : 5.

"Joan," she said, "your lack of fully trusting Him makes me believe that you are holding back part of your heart for yourself and not completely letting God take over your life."

It was true. I had come to Hollywood and seeing all the familiar names of the studios, there were still dreams of becoming an international star, but it *was* for myself and I was not kidding anyone.

Together we prayed and turned all my ambitions over to Him. It was such a relief because my whole stay had been fraught with my own desires welling up inside me. I left Hollywood heading back to the East coast with a peace of mind concerning the future. I did not know what it was, but I simply was going to trust God from now on.

My next appearance was to be in Boston, Massachusetts, for seven days. Greeting me once more was Bill Brown, who had called me several times when I was in other cities. I was so glad to see him again and I knew this was going to be a wonderful week.

Allan Emery, who was chairman of the arrangements for showing *Souls in Conflict*, and his lovely wife, Marian, made us feel very welcome. Several times we visited their beautiful home overlooking the suburbs of Boston and the harbour. The role of Cupid was assigned to the Emery family and between film showings and interviews they always managed to get Bill and me together for some delightful tour of the city or a drive along the beautiful shores of Massachusetts.

It seemed Bill and I never had time for a date and the only way we could get to talk to one another was behind the screen while the film was showing! We talked about our lives, our backgrounds and what our aspirations and dreams were. All the time I felt a certain glow that I had never really known before.

One night I was praying in my room at the hotel telling the Lord how happy I would be to be completely in His work if it was not His will that I should ever marry.

"But," I said, "if it is Your will, Lord, I surely would love to be married to someone like Bill Brown!"

Later that week, after the showing was over, Bill and I talked in the lobby of the hotel well past midnight. We were the only ones left, apart from the night porter, but we still had so much to talk about. Bill was telling me all about his family.

He said, "My sisters have had so many boy friends propose and I have heard them turn these guys down. I would hate to ask a girl to marry me and have her turn me down as that would probably give me an inferiority complex for the rest of my life. If I were going to marry someone, I sure would like her to be like you."

With that I impulsively said, "Why don't you practise on me?!"

So he asked me to marry him and from then on the memories are hazy, but I do remember saying "YES!" (To this day he still insists he was only practising!)

He phoned his family in Philadelphia who advised him to "Keep your feet on the ground, Billy!" They were concerned about his British actress sweeping their young brother off his feet. They really were justified in their caution, for we had only known each other for five weeks.

The showing of the film in Boston was extended for another week and we had seven more glorious days together. It seemed like a fairytale city to me and I did not care any more that the British had been defeated there. One Briton had scored a victory and that was enough for me. We had become engaged on November 11 — Armistice Day!

Allan Emery took us to a jeweller where we chose a ring. Bill had very little savings, so Allan offered to make a loan with Bill paying him back gradually. It took several years of $5 and $10 payments and we were so grateful for Allan's kind gesture and the trust he had in us.

At the end of our stay I had to say goodbye to Bill as we both had to go to separate cities with the film for a while. I flew to Washington. It was so hard to part and I could not take my eyes off the ring as I sat in the plane remembering all that had happened, so very quickly. Henrietta Mears had told me to commit my way unto the Lord and trust in Him and He would bring it to pass.

"I never dreamed it would be so quickly, dear Lord!"

Once in Washington, I was caught up again with all the arrangements for the première at Constitution Hall. That night for the first time as I spoke, I told publicly of my wanting to commit suicide. Before, I had never mentioned it as I was afraid it would upset my family.

After the showing, a young man told me how that night he had become so desperate with all the seemingly unsolvable problems in his life, he had decided to end it all. Walking the streets, he had wandered into the showing. Hearing me tell of God's love in my life and of how He had come in at a time when I was desperate, too, and thinking suicide was the only answer, the young man decided to try again and he gave his life to the Lord. This incident was an answer to a prayer of mine as I had wrestled with the fact of keeping my intended suicide a secret. The news reached the papers in England and now everyone knew that Joan Winmill had once contemplated taking her life. I ached for my family but hoped they would understand. Some didn't and it took many years to break down the barriers.

One night after a film showing, I had dinner with Bobby and Ethel Kennedy and Senator Henry Jackson. They were so interested in the film and in what had happened to me. I found myself telling them everything that had transpired.

Ethel said, "How wonderful you really feel that Christ is with you personally, wherever you go."

I assured her that this was so and that now I knew I could count on Him whatever the circumstances in my life. The circumstances that were to come about in her life, the tragic and futile violence which would wipe out their happiness together, I know brought her even closer to the Lord and because of His grace she has been able to carry on so courageously.

In Proverbs 31:10–11 it says, "Who can find a virtuous woman? for her price is far above rubies. The heart of her husband doth safely trust in her . . ."

Bobby found a virtuous wife and mother of his children in Ethel. I am thankful they enjoyed such happiness together, even though it was to be terminated so tragically. I am thankful too that Ethel has said she does not live without the hope of seeing him again.

14

NEXT ON MY agenda was Charlotte, North Carolina, and I would be staying in the home of Grady and Wilma Wilson. Grady had been a childhood friend of Billy Graham's and had travelled extensively with him as an Associate Evangelist. Grady met me at the airport and told me he had one stop to make before going home—the butcher's. I waited in the car as Grady went in to make his purchase and he came out grinning from ear to ear with a big bundle of steaks.

"I've got you the biggest steak in the South," he said. "We'll barbecue it when we get home."

Since becoming engaged I had completely lost my appetite, so I hoped I could eat this huge piece of meat that had been thrown onto what looked to me like a miniature bonfire.

We all sat down to eat and I was dying to tell Grady and Wilma the news about Bill and me. I took one bite out of the steak—a piece of meat that during the war would have lasted our whole family a week. That bite was all I could eat because of Bill Brown and I burst out the news to them.

Grady often regales me with this story of an English girl who toyed with the best steak in North Carolina because she was IN LOVE!

After my stay in Charlotte, I had been invited to spend

some time with Ruth Graham and rest there for a while before going on again to any more showings.

I stayed a month and during that time realised even more why the Lord had brought Ruth and Billy together. She was so exceptional. The children were very young, so she had five very busy little souls all clamouring for attention and Billy was away so much of the time. She seemed equipped to meet any situation or crisis that kept their warm, rustic Early American home in a constant state of perpetual motion. Children, dogs, phones and visitors caused this house to resound with the vigorous noises of sheer exuberant living.

Ruth gave me a room away from all the family noise and it was a chance to recuperate and learn some lessons in everyday living from a person who in a completely unaffected way had grown to know the joy of constant communion with the living Christ.

Of course there would be frequent knocks on my door and in would bound the children who clambered on to my bed, asking to be read to—so they could listen to this lady with "the funny accent".

Ruth's quiet talks by the log fire each night, after all the children were in bed, were locked in the secret place of my heart until I would have need to remember their deeper meaning and realise their value. Her Bible seemed to be part of her, always visible—open—waiting to be read, in whatever room she was.

"When the children were born," she said, "I found I could no longer set a certain hour for reading the Bible. I would get up earlier and earlier in the morning, but it seemed when I did there would always be a little one needing attention. So I decided to take my Bible with me whereever I was working and if I were able to read a few verses at a time I would still be guided and encouraged by His Word."

113

When my own children came, I remembered this and it was often the secret to being able to have that quiet flow of communication with the Lord.

Ruth never gave the appearance of feeling sorry for herself with Billy away so much, even though I know she missed him terribly. The only time I ever saw her a little down was one day, seated by the fireplace once more, she read a letter from a missionary she had not heard from since her college days.

The letter read, "You probably don't remember me, Ruth, now you are the wife of such a famous evangelist. It must be a very glamorous life. My husband and I are stuck here on the mission field."

Ruth looked up and I saw a tear in her eye as she said, "At least she is with her husband."

She put the letter away and quickly resumed her many tasks.

Bill flew down to see me and stayed at the local inn. I had told Ruth all about him and she told me she was concerned we did not really know each other very well. Then she saw his photograph and said, "Anyone who looks so much like Cliff Barrows has got to be all right!"

Bill made a hit with her immediately. The children adored him and delighted in spying on us. Bunny, who was very small, perceptively said, complete with thumb in mouth, "I think Uncle Bill *loves* Aunt Joan!"

Ruth lent us Billy's car and Montreat was a wonderful place to court. We drove through the beautiful mountains and forests and my heart was so grateful to the Lord for all this happiness. I was sure I would just burst one day from sheer joy.

One night while parked by the entrance to Montreat, we were deep in discussion (or something) when a car pulled up behind us. It was the patrol car making a routine check but

Bill started the engine up so fast and roared out of there. Later he said it must have looked terrible—Billy's car with another man in it. The patrol officer might have thought he was with Ruth! She laughed about it when we got home.

Later that night, while reading my daily chapter of Proverbs, this verse hit my eye: "The wicked flee when no man pursueth!"

Now came the time to meet Bill's family officially in Philadelphia. We flew back from Montreat together as I was to appear with the film in that historic city of the Liberty Bell. They were all at the airport to greet us and I felt just like a buck private at his first drill session—really getting an inspection! Little Gayle, Bill's niece, listened to my accent for a moment and said, "Why does she talk Russian, Mom?"

At dinner that night around the family table everyone talked and I waited for an interval to be able to say something profound—to make a good impression—but there never was an interval, everyone kept right on! (Bill told me afterwards that they thought I was rather quiet.) My grandmother's training had always been that you waited until someone finished speaking before you chimed in. I have revised this teaching now and jump right in with the rest of them. It took a few years to get used to this vital family and I have grown to love them all. Then too, they have grown to love this English girl who always seems to go through life in low gear (compared to them!).

Film showings had been scheduled all over England and Scotland, so I had to fly back and leave Bill for a while. I have never understood why Shakespeare wrote "Parting is such sweet sorrow"—it was anything but sweet. At the airport Bill gave me a beautiful little compact with a music box in it which played "I Love You Truly". I loved it so much that I played it over and over again until finally the mechanism slowed down and it sounded like "Short'nin' Bread".

Being in England again brought all the problems of my past back before me. The Press continued to trail me. The weeks went by and I was becoming a wreck from all the hounding. By the time I was to return to America, I left England distraught, overtired and sad.

Daddy came to see me off and pressed a little box into my hand.

"Open it when you are on the plane," he said.

It was hard to say goodbye to him. Kissing him, I then turned and ran to the plane, feeling so torn inside. As my foot left English soil I wondered when I would be back in this country I loved so much. Once I boarded the plane I sat praying for Daddy, for his state of health was always causing him pain and discomfort.

Remembering the little box I reached down into my hand-bag and unwrapped it carefully. Inside was a small, beauti-ful gold cross with a card written in Daddy's handwriting.

"Keep this remembrance of our Lord close to you. It will lessen the miles between us as we think how much He loves us both. Your ever-loving Daddy."

The tears that ran down my face as I looked out of the window were tears of parting and tears of joy. Since I had become a Christian Daddy had never been able to talk to me about the Lord. He had been so difficult to witness to be-cause he was such a kind, gentle man, always helping others. He put me to shame. I had explained to him that because of our inherent sinful nature, none of us was worthy of God's love. He had listened and said, "I'm glad for you dear, that you have found such peace through Him."

Then the subject would change, but now as I sat looking at the cross and the card, I knew it was his way of showing me that he had at last acknowledged his need too of our Lord. Perhaps in no other way would he have been able to express himself.

Back in the States, everything picked up momentum. I was to stay with Bill's sister, Eva, for a few days until I got my schedule. Bill had news now that he was being transferred to the West Coast and this would mean our being separated once more. Suddenly we decided to be married immediately so that I could be with him in California. The whole family went to work on this monumental project. It was Monday and we made plans to be married on Thursday evening.

I can hardly believe that in four days our church wedding was planned. Bill's mother flew up to Philadelphia from her home in Florida. For the first time I met this lady I had heard so much about from Bill. I knew right away why Bill loved and respected her, for even though she had suffered so many hardships she always showed the love of Christ. Widowed, with six children in school, her complete dependence had been on her Saviour, who had given her comfort and strength through the years. She accepted me into her family with such love; I felt very privileged to be her daughter-in-law.

I was married in a white wedding dress found on a sale rack, but which fitted me perfectly. As a result of telephoning there were over two hundred people at the wedding! And, too, instead of cake and punch in a church basement the guests were invited to a beautiful reception given for us in the lovely home of Fred and Millie Dienert. It was hard to believe how gracious these new-found Christian friends were to two bewildered but desperately happy people. I remember having to walk down that long aisle on my own. I missed my father's arm to lean on. How happy he would have been to see me married, but finances and the short notice made it impossible for him to be there.

As Bill and I took our vows I realised the great solemnity of that moment. These were promises to God that we were

117

making. Here we stood, two people from very different backgrounds, brought up thousands of miles apart: yet all along God knew we would one day be led together and become one.

After the reception at the Dienert's house I had to go back and help Bill sort out his whole bedroom. He had not had time even to think of it, and here we were leaving for California immediately. In the middle of the packing he remembered he had not phoned for a reservation at a hotel for that night. It was now two in the morning and when the hotel clerk answered, he couldn't understand whether Bill was wanting a room for the middle of that night or the next night! When we finally arrived at the hotel at four-thirty, two weary bodies stood by the desk and except for my drooping orchid I am sure the clerk never dreamed that here was a honeymoon couple!

We left for California the next morning, bleary-eyed. Each day we would try to travel over five hundred miles. I can tell you—it was not the ideal way to spend a honeymoon!

We arrived in Los Angeles and then came the job of apartment hunting. After much searching we managed to find a little apartment in Van Nuys. It was not palatial by any means, but it was clean. We found the little, bird-like, whitehaired landlady was in our flat all the time making sure we were being good tenants. A bang on the bathroom wall from her adjoining flat would indicate that she thought we had run enough bath water. After a while I began to feel she really lived with us, especially when we were told not to close any kitchen cabinets after ten p.m. as the noise of them closing kept her awake. There was wall-to-wall carpeting in the kitchen, the variety that seemed to delight in eating up every stain and greedily held on to it no matter what one did to clean it. This had been put down so that our footsteps wouldn't bother her. Each time Bill went out he slammed the screen door behind him and one day, when we returned, the screen door had been taken off its hinges and it was now open season for all the flies and mosquitoes to invade our house. The weather that summer zoomed to 110 degrees for over a week!

Now we were living right next to Hollywood and Bill was the film representative for the area. It sounded very glamorous to those back in England who would write saying, "Well, you finally made it, you are lucky, Joan!" Oh, how I longed for London, with its transportation. Here, stuck in the San Fernando Valley and not being able to drive, I had to rely on Bill for everything.

The apartment was so hot, we finally managed to get enough money to buy a small, revolving fan from the Salvation Army Thrift Store that wobbled around precariously; but at least it helped move the air. Bill was earning very little money at this time, but it did not seem to worry us. We were happy together and could laugh at the eccentricities of the landlady, even when she walked into our bedroom one morning thinking we had already left for church and was greeted by Bill in his birthday suit!

However, I was not the greatest housekeeper. Acting did not equip me too well for marriage and its responsibilities and my trips to the supermarket were often a disaster, especially as I did not know many of the brand names sold there. Bill would watch me cook and keep saying, "We just don't cook like that in America, honey!"

We didn't in England either, but I had to learn somehow and it was mostly by trial and error I began trying to make any kind of semblance of order to our little flat and the meals I hesitatingly served. Bill (luckily) had been born with a cast-iron stomach.

I remember saying to Bill, "You know, I don't know how

119

people stay married without the Lord, do you?"

"Surely it hasn't been that bad, has it?" he asked incredulously.

We laughed and thanked Him for being able to come to Him with all our problems and, too, with all our happiness together.

My conservative English background left me so much to accept of American life. Especially when Bill would pull up in some little town, roll down the window of the car, and yell, "Hey, buddy—where's the First Baptist Church?!"

He was no more his buddy than the man in the moon.

We made many friends in the Los Angeles area, renewing some friendships like Dick Ross. Our stay there was a happy one, in spite of all the mistakes we made—but they were made together and that was wonderful to me. Our time was spent at so many showings of *Souls in Conflict*, Bill sometimes booking us for twenty-nine screenings a month. It was heartening for me to see the Lord continue to work through this medium, sometimes in very small meetings which contradicted any critics who would say it was the hypnosis of the large crowds that so often caused people to respond. It was that quiet inner need that responded—that quiet need that is basically within everyone if they will only acknowledge it.

During this time we received some wonderful news. John had given his life to Christ at Wembley Stadium in London, during a Billy Graham Crusade there! Bill and I were overjoyed as we heard how God had worked. John, with reporters and photographers, had been all set to punch Billy on the jaw but instead Billy had reached out and shaken his hand! They were then able to sit and talk and John responded to Christ after seeing the sincerity of this man who had such a calling from God to tell others of the Gospel of Jesus Christ.

Recently Bill and I were asked to appear on a TV talk show along with John, who now lives in America and travels all over the country with his own Christian drama group. On camera the three of us expressed our love for Christ.

Sometimes I look back on our lives, on how John and I met—two people with a longing in our souls that only God could satisfy. The turmoil and anguish that surrounded our relationship was really a heartcry for help and a deep basic desire to be loved.

I am glad that for many years John, too, has no longer been alone.

15

WITH MY HEALTH record, I did not seem a very good risk for motherhood. Two nervous breakdowns did not qualify me as a very suitable candidate for this responsible and arduous role.

Bill loved children and I can remember in Atlanta, Georgia, after a showing of *Souls in Conflict*, I had watched him talk to a group of them who had come forward at the invitation to accept Christ as their Saviour. He took so much time with them and they obviously adored him.

I loved children, but only other people's. I did not want to be tied down to more responsibilities, especially when we were travelling around so much and not sure what our future held. Basically, the nagging fear of my mother's death in childbirth haunted me.

Knowing how much Bill wanted a child, I began to really pray about it, pouring all my fears out to the Lord. The more I thought about it, the more I realised I was not trusting Him as far as my wellbeing was concerned. I had trusted Him to take care of me when flying, but the act of childbirth which had been going on for so many centuries I continued to wrestle with! After all, He had created me. I only had to believe He would be with me as He had promised.

It seems that each time there is an important step in my

life I have to wrestle everything out with the Lord, and this time was no exception. But He answered my prayers, and recorded in my old red Bible are these words:

October 6, 1955—   I pray that if it is His will, soon we will have a child.
"Fear not for thy prayer is heard!" Luke 1:13

July 16, 1956—   William Frederick Brown, Jr. born
"For this child I prayed; and the Lord hath given me my petition which I asked of Him . . ."
1 Samuel 1:27, 28

Three years later, I was to write underneath this entry:

November 22, 1959—   David Stewart Brown born
"Lo, children are an heritage of the Lord . . ."
Psalm 127:3

What a heritage! These two sons have brought Bill and me such joy and continue to do so. Oh, there are times when I still wonder if I shall ever make it as a mother and have to cry out to God to give me wisdom to deal with the many-faceted problems. But I would not change my role as a mother for anything else.

Recalling my very real fears whilst I carried each of my sons brings me closer to the Lord as I see how much He took care of me.

Bill decided it was time to leave California and head back East, but our bank account did not agree. So we decided to work our way back by taking some film showings in towns across the country, gradually making our way to Florida.

This sounded good in theory but in practice it was another matter!

We did not have enough money to stay at motels, so Bill thought it a great idea to buy a caravan.

I had seen luxurious caravans in their sales parks along the highway and imagined it would be fun to pull one. However, the price tags for these modern wheeled homes were way over our heads. Bill said we would have to look for a used one in the local "For Sale" ads. "Well," I thought, "a used one wouldn't be bad if the owner has taken good care of it."

Imagine my amazement when my dear husband took me to a little place in the San Fernando Valley and showed me the caravan we *could* afford—for $110. I took one look at it —a crate on wheels. But Bill told me to imagine how it would look after he had painted it. My imagination didn't help. I envisioned a *repainted* crate on wheels! Inside was even worse. The old gentleman living in it had not kept it up at all but, "The basics are there," said Bill, "and look, it has a cupboard so we can hang our clothes and they won't get creased!" "The eternal optimist," I thought as I surveyed the cramped quarters that were going to be home for a few months.

Bill repainted the exterior and the interior. He got so carried away that he painted the inside of the refrigerator with the same paint he had used for the rest of the caravan, the result being that our food tasted and smelled of paint for the whole trip. Friends donated all kinds of accoutrements with which to furnish our new home, even making curtains— which helped considerably. As we left, the staff of World Wide Pictures, wives and loved ones came to see us pull away in our vintage home on wheels. Someone remarked, "At least you're not pregnant, Joan." Guess what? I was!

To make things worse, on our first night out, we be-

124

friended a stray dog as another travelling companion.

Bill had written ahead to towns in all the different States we would go through on our way back East. Some, like New Mexico, he had mapped us going around in circles as we showed the film in such towns as Albuquerque, Tucumcari, and Alamagordo. With a cross-country schedule of three months, here we were with many miles to go, many showings to attend, and I was getting larger by the hour! Luckily I had a pink tweed suit with a Chanel type jacket, so I could hide the fact for a while. After holding together my skirt with a safety pin which graduated in size each week, it finally became necessary to use a large mattress pin to hold body and soul together! My legs were exceedingly swollen and looked like tree trunks.

In one town when I had been introduced to speak, I walked past a group of ladies and overheard one of them say, "My, doesn't she have an extraordinary figure for an actress!"

What my husband had done in setting up these showings was to write a letter to the local minister in each town and say his church could have the film *Souls in Conflict* on a certain night. Without saying we were married, in order to get the minister to accept, Bill would write, "By the way, the star of the film can be in your town on that date and would be able to make a personal appearance." Once they accepted, Bill would write back and say, "By the way, the star of the film is my wife." This backfired on us in one town as the second letter never reached the minister. After arriving and meeting the minister Bill said, "Before the showing, Joan and I want to get back to the caravan to rest together." The poor man finally had to tell Bill he just did not think it was right to be carrying on like this while being in the ministry for the Lord!

One day the towing hitch broke as we were heading down

the highway. Our dishes went flying and the whole interior was a mess of dog food and our food. All Bill could say was, "But honey, our clothes are still hanging up in the cupboard." Oh, that cupboard; you would think it was the answer to everything!

The smell of the butane gas when I awakened in the morning with morning sickness, plus the smell of the stray dog and food, was enough to make me throw up everything. Bill and I shared a bed that only measured thirty-nine inches across and was as hard as a board. To top it all off, one night a minister was taking me to do a TV show and turning to talk to me he rammed right into the back of another car. My face hit the windscreen, which shattered. After pulling myself together, the driver being in shock, I managed to stumble into a bar with blood running down my face and ask for help. The juke box was playing full tilt and people were running around trying to help me. I was cleaned up, shot into another car, whisked to the TV station and presented as the English actress who was appearing with her latest film. My chin was very swollen and there were superficial scratches on my face. The whole picture was not a glamorous one, plus "the extraordinary figure". After the show, I was taken to the hospital and X-rayed and pronounced well enough to continue our journeys. The result of the accident was that I now had a huge bruised double chin, plus scars on my face to add to the rotund figure in a bursting pink tweed suit.

Morning sickness seeemed to last all day with me and after the long trip I was thankful to arrive at Bill's mother's house in West Palm Beach. Mom took great care of me and it was wonderful to rest after all those meetings. I bought a pre-natal care book and learned it was best not to travel while expecting! We had travelled three thousand miles and there were quite a few to go before we could settle, so I chose to ignore these warnings.

We left the caravan at Bill's mother's, where she later was able to sell it for us to some gypsies at a handsome profit of $55. I was never so glad to get rid of any possession in my life.

Bill had now been loaned by Billy Graham to Howard Butt, the popular businessman-evangelist, for several months so he could help set up Crusades in the South. We lived in Macon, Georgia, for a few months near a paper factory. The smell was unbelievable, even if one were not expecting! Then on to Greensboro, North Carolina, finally getting to Montgomery, Alabama, where I now could await the birth of my first child. We rented a furnished home and while Bill raced around making arrangements for another Crusade I pottered around looking like a barge in full sail, preparing clothes for the imminent arrival of our baby (who did not choose to make an appearance at the prophesied time).

The doctor decided after three extra weeks of waiting that it was time to induce the birth. I was to awaken at six the next morning, take a large bottle of castor oil immediately, then enter the hospital.

When the alarm went off and I saw the bottle of castor oil awaiting me, I groaned. I did not want to face this day, but if there is one thing that having a baby teaches you—you cannot run away. It is inevitable that something will have to happen!

I arrived at the hospital, kissed Bill goodbye (as he was due on a radio programme and had a myriad of tasks ahead of him) then staggered in to face whatever lay before me.

By now a peace had come over me and I just knew I could trust God to take care of me. I thought of Mary and how she had had to travel before the birth of Jesus. What rough roads she journeyed over before reaching an inn that had no room. There were no kind nurses waiting for her, only a stable that was to be her maternity room. Her faith inspired me as I realised how fortunate I was to have a doctor who was genuinely concerned for his patient. Dr Dorrough stayed with me all day, always by my side when the going started to get rough. In between whiffs of twilight sleep ("Your Queen used this at the birth of her children"), he would whisper words of encouragement. I learned afterwards that he had cancelled all appointments for that day. He knew of my mother's death and said, "You were away from your family and I wanted to do everything I could to help at this time." The Lord had surely touched the heart of this overwhelmingly busy doctor so that I could be comforted instead of fearful.

Billy (William Frederick Brown, Jnr.) was finally born at 9.30 p.m., ten pounds and a quarter ounce. A huge bouncing boy, with an expression on his face that seemed to say, "All right, world, I finally made it!" He did not look a newborn baby but at least a month old!

What a miracle, I thought, as I held him in my arms with Bill beside me. I find it hard to understand how any woman cannot believe in God when she looks for the first time into the face of the new creation she has been carrying within her for nine months. I found it awesome as I watched little Bill sleeping contentedly, oblivious of the joy his arrival had given us.

To include in each birth announcement, Bill had a small card printed that read:

My Son

I saw you for the first time today. The nurse held you up so that I could get a good look at you through the nursery window. There wasn't much of you that I could see, but I felt very proud. You were my son!

I was proud and thankful too—thankful to God for you, thankful that you were well and strong, with your tiny body in proper working order. Your mother and I had prayed that it might be so. And seeing you as you were today was the answer to our prayers.

And there were other things we had prayed about, things we shall continue to pray about as you grow up. That our words and our lives may lead you to know the Saviour that we know. That you may not only belong to us, but to Him. For we know of nothing better than a life in Christ, and we wish the best for you.

I learned, upon arriving home, that we would be moving in three weeks. Bill had been asked to go to New York to help set up the scheduled Crusade that Billy Graham would be holding in Madison Square Garden.

We packed up to move to New York and I felt mad at the world. I was so tired and here I was having to move out of this house with a newborn baby.

"Well, Lord, please don't ever let this happen again. If I ever have another child I want to be settled and have time to enjoy him, not all this confounded packing."

On our way to New York, we stopped at Montreat to see Billy and Ruth Graham and to stay at Ruth's parents' house. Dr and Mrs Bell were two of the dearest Christians I have ever met.

It was in their home, before I was married, that I had spent my first American Thanksgiving. I shall never forget the warmth of their friendliness, the glow of their home and the tremendous feeling of thanksgiving that came over me as I sat at the table with all their family to celebrate a holiday that was completely foreign to me.

Now I was in their home once more, a wife and a mother.

One evening we went up the mountain to the Grahams'
house and asked Billy to dedicate Bill Junior to the Lord.
For this Anglican it was a real compromise, as I always
secretly hoped he would be christened with a beautiful
white robe in a stained glass-windowed church surrounded
by my family and Bill's. But it was a beautiful service in
their living room, and it holds a very special place in our
hearts. After Billy dedicated him to the Lord, Ruth looked
at the sleeping baby and said, "Why, look—he's dead to the
world."

We stayed a year in New York and I began to experience
the tremendous adjustment mothers go through when suddenly confined to their homes with a baby. The frustration
was mixed with guilt because of wanting to be able to be
free to go out when I wanted to. Oh, there were so many
happy times in New York with Bill Junior, watching him
grow, responding to love, seeing him smile. We lived in a
section that did not have a park and the only "safe" area to
walk was around the block of the apartment building. It was
sad to see to many derelicts and drunks on the street. Often
I would have to push the pram around them as they lay on
the pavement sleeping off the effects of the alcohol.

One day in a drugstore one staggered over to me and
said, "What a beautiful baby you have," then burst out
crying. Bending down to Bill Junior, he said to him, "Never
become like me, son. I'm a wino and I've wasted my life."
It was heartbreaking to see this shell of a man and I stood
and talked with him for a while telling him that his life was
not hopeless, that God loved him no matter what had happened before in his life. He grabbed my hands and thanked
me and then was gone into the maze of humanity once more.
I often wonder what became of him and whether he ever
really asked the Lord to come into his life and help him.
Standing there I could not judge that scarred human being,

for what circumstances had brought him to the excruciating loneliness that must have been his constant companion? Only the cheap alcohol that blotted out the agonising memories was his gruesome comrade, and was gradually destroying this man who once had been a little boy like mine.

Bill's work next took us to Australia and little Bill loved the koala bears, kangaroos and also the kookaburra that lived in a tree outside his bedroom window. Each morning he would be awakened by the laughing sound of this delightful bird.

I shall never forget the communion service Bill and I attended one Sunday at Donald Begbie's church in a suburb of Sydney. Never have I heard the words of the Anglican Communion service spoken with more feeling and when I took the bread and the wine I was brought to a deepening consciousness of the sacrifice of our Lord. "This is my body, broken for YOU . . ." So often I had taken this service for granted but again I was reminded of all it really means. Jesus's willingness to die on that Cross, paying such a price, makes communion the most costly meal in history. It was an act of love that would surpass anything else that could possibly come into my life.

To see so many thousands of people giving their lives to this Saviour at the Sydney Crusade was intensely moving.

During our stay Bill made a lengthy trip to New Zealand to make arrangements for meetings there, so I was left alone with Bill Junior. Always I disliked the thought of Bill flying and the Lord had to reassure me over and over again that He was taking care of him. I decided to find out the exact times of take off and arrival in each city so I could pray the plane up and then safely down again. I even set an alarm so I would not miss it!

Little Bill had a sandbox on the porch and I loved to sit and watch him play. The day Bill left, a white dove flew into the porch and nestled in a gable. It was a beautiful creature and very simplistically, to me it seemed the Lord's way of telling me everything was going to be all right with Bill. The day of his return the dove flew away never to come back again.

However, when Bill returned I told him I had set an alarm and had prayed his plane up and down safely. He thanked me but said, "Honey, I hate to tell you this but New Zealand is in a different time zone. It's an hour ahead of here!"

While I had been busily praying, the plane had already taken off and landed! "Well," I thought, "the Bible promises that the Lord will answer our prayers even before we ask."

When our days in Australia were over, we said a regretful goodbye to so many people who had become close friends and we began our long trip back home, via England.

Now I was expecting another baby, but I was not to be deterred from visiting as many countries as possible on our way back.

It was an incredible trip. We stopped off in New Guinea, Manila and then Hong Kong. I was saddened at the sight of so much poverty next door to the luxurious hotels. It was there in Kowloon that we met two modern-day disciples for Christ—Archdeacon and Mrs Donnithorne from England, missionaries who had had to leave mainland China when the Communists took over. They were both elderly then, but thought nothing of climbing to the rooftops of the tall buildings that housed refugees to have services for the children, teaching them about Jesus and the basics of reading, writing and arithmetic. The tall, venerable Archdeacon could be seen striding through the old Walled City where the couple had started a home for elderly ladies. When our plane left for India, the Archdeacon walked all the way to the airport to bring me some preserved ginger because he knew I liked it. He has now gone to be with his beloved Christ; but Mrs Donnithorne, although crippled with arthritis and having had major surgery, still climbs to the rooftops and teaches the children. These are the Christians whose lives shine with a radiance that the awesome problems of this world can never dim.

Boarding the plane, I remember thinking, "Good, it has Rolls-Royce engines—we'll be safe with them." Little Bill enjoyed looking out of the window as we took off from Hong Kong airport and were then bound for India.

Half-an-hour outside Calcutta, we ran into a very bad thunderstorm. I looked out of the window but could see nothing except rain beating on the glass. Stewardesses were now moving up and down the aisles, taking down any luggage that had been left overhead.

We made our descent, swerving in the high winds, when suddenly there was a huge crash and with a tremendous lurch, the plane ascended once more.

Bill Junior said very calmly, "I think the big bad wolf is going to make this plane crash!" Wonderful words when you are in a blinding storm!

"If this is true," I thought, "my life should start to appear before my eyes." But nothing happened, in fact my mind went a complete blank—at first I could not even remember a verse of scripture. Then the verse in Psalm 37 came to my mind, the one that Miss Henrietta Mears had prayed with me in Hollywood: "Commit thy way unto the Lord, trust also in Him and He will bring it to pass."

I kept repeating it over and over again. I did commit us all to Him and prayed He would bring this aircraft down safely. The pilot started another approach for landing and we all held on, white knuckled and breathing heavily. Again there was a huge crash and then we bumped onto the landing strip with a huge jolt. What a relief. We were down! Bill

133

undid his seat belt and relaxed. I was still holding Bill Junior wide-eyed, so thankful to be on terra firma. But suddenly the terra was not so firma as we began to bump and get shot all over the plane. The brakes had failed and the plane was lurching across a soggy rice field, which finally brought it to a halt.

The pilot rushed out of his cabin and brushed past us to look out of the window at the engines, making sure they were not going to catch fire.

We were told to stay in our seats, but the men were to get off first. "I always thought it was women and children first," I said to Bill Junior as I busily got our raincoats on. A calm had descended over me that was not of my own making, for I had committed our way to the Lord and again He had taken care of us.

The men were needed to hoist out the canvas chute and finally we were all able to be pushed down it to the safety of the muddy field. I wondered about snakes, but tried to think about something else. Fifteen minutes later the ambulances, crash wagons and fire engines arrived. It was a comforting sight! We were boarded onto a bus and taken to the main terminal of Dum-Dum airport. "A good name," I thought.

After the fright of it was over, it was so funny to see all the fellow passengers traipsing around with mud stains over their ankles. You could easily tell who had been on the ill-fated flight.

We were told that one wing had hit a tree on the first attempt to land and the other wing had hit a tree as we landed. What saved us were the Rolls-Royce engines that were strong enough to send the plane up the second time.

"Thank you Rolls-Royce and thank you Lord."

We were taken to a hotel for the night and perhaps the drive there in the taxi was more frightening than the crash. The doors were done up with string and the driver never seemed to look where he was going as he swerved amongst people walking in the streets. The only time he seemed to be really conscious of his surroundings was when he had to slow down to avoid a sacred cow.

I could not believe the sight of these people as I looked out of the taxi window and saw so many men and young boys preparing to sleep on the streets. Each day many die and are carted away, forgotten, making space for more hungry desolate souls.

When we left Australia we had not intended to stay overnight in India as, with its heat, we felt it better for me to stop in a cooler country. I am glad we had to stop there for it no longer made India a statistic to me, with all its heartache and hunger and the humiliation of the masses as each day they had to forage for food in order to exist. It would not be enough for me to walk through the streets saying to them "Jesus loves you" when all around was stench and poverty I had never known before. To reach these dear souls for Christ would take acts of mercy such as He had shown. It would take the dedication of someone like Sister Teresa who has dedicated her life to them and opened a Home for the Dying. Among all the heartache, she goes on giving hope and love to so many.

As we left Calcutta the next day, I looked out of our plane window and saw the wreck of our ill-fated Comet way in the distance, still standing there like a wounded bird, its wings broken.

Abruptly my thoughts turned to the child I was carrying within me. I had taken for granted we were all safe yesterday, but would there be damage to this little growing soul? The impact had been jarring to my whole body—could it precipitate a miscarriage? I began to pray again that everything would be all right.

16

In Indianapolis I enrolled in natural childbirth classes, having read so much about the method. After Bill Junior's birth, I had felt cheated somehow and wanted to be conscious so that I could welcome my second baby into the world.

I looked around at all the fellow walruses puffing and blowing on the floor as we exercised and laughed. Most of them were so serious in their attempts at grace at a time like this. I learned that our instructor, Carol Bonham, was a Christian who was taking counselling classes for the Billy Graham Crusade. A friendship was established and here once again God had reached down and said, "You are not without friends in a strange city, because there are those who love Me here . . ."

The day before the baby was to arrive I decided I would probably have to go through the same ordeal as I did with Bill Junior—wait for another month and then have to have the baby induced. Going to bed that night I decided motherhood was overrated!

Sunday morning dawned and we all got up and went to church, heaving me in and out of our car. I rested for most of the day and felt very sorry for myself. In the evening we all watched *Lassie*, it being Bill Junior's favourite programme. Then I began to suddenly have pains. I thought it was something I had eaten, but they got worse and I staggered into the bathroom. Three-year-old Bill came in after me and wanted to know what was wrong.

"Not feeling too good, Mother? 'Dennis the Menace' is coming on next, Mom, and that will make you feel better!"

I realised my own little "Dennis" was on the way and I yelled out to Bill to get the car. He telephoned a friend to come and stay with Bill Junior. It was snowing and I was sure we would never make it to the hospital in time. We sped down the road to the hospital, slipping and sliding, praying and praying.

At the hospital, after the forms were signed, I kissed Bill goodbye and was whisked in a wheelchair into an elevator and then began the countdown. Less than half-an-hour later I was wheeled into the delivery room. Trying to remember all my exercises for relaxing I was greeted by the anaesthetist asking if I wanted a nice whiff to set me off to sleep. I told him I didn't, for the Lord had assured me it was going to be all right.

In a mirror, I saw my second son born and it was a moment that I shared with the Lord. I cried out to Him my thankfulness and praise that He had again entrusted me with one of His creations. There was pain, but it was bearable knowing that as I worked with the doctor the miracle of birth was being enacted and I was part of the incredible production that was God's.

I held my little son in my arms as they wheeled me out of the delivery room.

The young intern who had been present came and asked if he could talk with me for a while. He sat by my bed and said, "I've seen many births now and I have heard women scream and curse God for the pain, but you were praising Him. I wonder if birth shouldn't always be like that?"

I was able to tell him that Jesus was so close to me in that

137

delivery room and that it was the most natural thing in the world for me to want to thank Him for my little son. Then, too, I was able to tell him that basically I am a coward— terrified of anything to do with a hospital or pain. But it was His grace that took my fears away and made the birth of my child a beautiful and glorious experience.

"He shall gently lead those that are with young . . ." Isaiah 40:11.

He had gently led me over many thousands of miles, calmed all my fears and had given me two sons to bring us joy.

We called the baby David after the Psalmist and I prayed the same prayer that I did when Bill Junior was born:

"Lord, this child is a gift from You. Help me to love him, care for him, teach him of Your great love and then when the time comes to let him go out in the world, give me Your grace and strength not to hold on to him!'"

This prayer proves harder as the years go by. "To let him go . . ." Our sons have become so much a part of our lives, it would be very easy for me to play the role of the possessive mother. But Bill and I realise we are merely custodians of their lives here on earth only until they reach the age when they must stand alone.

Above all, I have tried to teach them that they will never be alone for no matter what the situation, Christ, who has come into their lives, will always be there.

Always. What a wonderful word that is when applied to His love.

Remember what I had told the Lord about being settled the next time I had a baby? Well here I was again in exactly the same predicament for we were to move to Philadelphia three weeks after David was born.

Trying to pack, still feeling very weak and with two children to care for, I had an award-winning attack of the blues that besiege most mothers after the birth of a child. But the Lord had foreseen my need and had already brought into my life someone who volunteered to help me. Ginny Booth had been working in the Crusade office and she took over so many tasks for me as I struggled to regain my strength and pack for the journey to Philadelphia. He knew I could never have made it without her. Ginny became Bill's secretary for quite some time and we all grew to love her as one of our family.

The day of departure dawned and I went to awaken Bill Junior early. I was horrified by what I saw—his face was covered with red, angry-looking spots. Measles had developed and now we would have to leave with a three-week-old baby and a sick child. What a journey to Philadelphia!

We had only been in Philadelphia a few months when one morning a telegram was delivered.

Opening it, I read: "Daddy died this morning. Please phone. Love, Ann."

I read it over and over to try to comprehend what the words meant. Only a few days before we had been planning that I would go to England with Billy and David, while Bill had to go on a trip to South America. This way Daddy would be able to meet his grandson, David, for the first time. I sat in shock trying to sort out the thoughts that crowded my mind. Daddy was dead and an indescribable agony of grief swept over me. To think I would not see his face again nor hear his voice welcoming his grandsons.

Bill, feeling my hurt, put his comforting arms around me and together we sobbed out our sorrow to Christ, locked together in the depths of anguish that grips everyone when they experience the loss of someone dear to them.

Through my tears I remembered that the night before as I was reading the Bible I had been struck by a verse in Revelation 14:13:

And I heard a voice from heaven saying unto me, Write, Blessed are the dead, which die in the Lord from hence-forth: Yea, saith the Spirit, that they may rest from their labours; and their works do follow them.

I had read this over and over wondering who the Lord might be bringing to my mind. There was no one I knew at that time who was ill and finally I dismissed the thoughts. Now as I sat shattered by the news of Daddy's passing, those words came back to comfort my heart.

Daddy *was* resting now and he had suffered so much over the years due to his health. His work kept him travelling over England in a car that had no heater and he often came home frozen from the long hours spent driving from city to city.

I called Ann. The overseas connection was not very clear, but I heard her say that Daddy had rushed over the road to a neighbour who had been found overcome by gas from an unlighted gas burner and, in rescuing her, he had suffered a fatal heart attack. Ann's voice sounded so desolate and I knew that she and Geraldine would feel so dreadfully alone without the love and care of my father. The terrible finality for them came shortly when the company he had been working for arrived to collect the car.

That night I sat by the window of the apartment watching the sunset. Watching, until the sun finally dropped out of view. Thinking of a man who in the world's estimation could not be termed a success. A few weeks earlier he had written me telling of the disappointment he had received in his work. The owner of the company had died and now younger men had stepped in and he was not to receive the promotion the owner had been promising him.

"I feel such a failure," he wrote. "I have not achieved all I had hoped."

His letter had moved me deeply and I had sat down and

written immediately telling him never to think of himself as a failure. We often compute success by how much we have in the bank, but how many men who had been able to make fortunes were always the kind of husbands or fathers they should have been? I told him that I was so grateful to the Lord for a father who always understood, who was always interested in all my activities. Though I hurt him in so many ways, his love was always unchanging, always there when I needed it. To me he epitomised success, for he was a man who never compromised to attain recognition but was ready to help anyone at any time.

"No, Daddy, you are not a failure. Please remember this and know how much I love you."

How thankful I was that I had not procrastinated (as is my habit) when writing letters, but had sent that letter to him.

Sitting there by the window I felt the Comforter that Christ said He would send, and the miles that had separated Daddy and I were no more for he was with Him and He was not even a breath away.

The next day I collected my mail and there was a letter in my father's familiar hand, written only a few days before he died. In it he asked just when he would be able to see his dear grandson, David, and remembered the happy times he had spent with Bill Junior. He said his thoughts and prayers were with us and his last words, "God bless you all" rang in my ears as I remembered the voice that had guided me over the years.

One day, months later, I began thinking of how much I would have loved to visit my father. Now he was dead; I badly missed his letters, always encouraging, that resounded with his endearing personality.

Standing by the sink in the kitchen, I suddenly said to the Lord, "Oh, if only Daddy were alive!"

141

And the heartache of my grief swept over me again.

"But he is! So much more than he has ever been!"

I looked up startled and then realised the Lord had given these thoughts to me. They flooded over me like a soothing balm and their comfort surrounded me.

"Thank you, Lord, of course he is," I said through my tears.

I thought of all the illness he had had—I could not wish him back. If only he could have met his other grandson it would have given him such pleasure. David would not know this gentle man with his delightful sense of humour and his great sense of loyalty to those he loved. But one day he will. What reunions we shall have with those we love in Christ. I often try to imagine our meeting again. Until then I have such wonderful memories.

One particular memory stands out. Shortly after my mother died, Daddy had taken me for a holiday at Selsey, in Sussex. We stayed in a little hotel overlooking the bay where, from our bedroom window, I could see the little boats and sea gulls and imagine all kinds of adventures that lay across the horizon.

A storm was brewing out to sea and I watched the black clouds rolling closer towards the shore. It began to rain as I got ready for bed. Daddy was downstairs talking to some of the other guests, when a huge flash of lightning followed by a deafening clap of thunder made the lights go out. Nanny had always told me that thunder was "God getting in the coals!" but this did not comfort me that night in the darkness of my strange bedroom. I began to cry, frightened, wondering where my father was. Then I heard his voice calling to me as he came up the stairs, "Don't be afraid, Joan. I'm here. Everything is all right."

The sound of his voice reassuring me took away all my fears and his presence once more in the bedroom enabled me to sleep peacefully, knowing he would protect me.

When we come to the point of death we will all need a shepherd. Just as Daddy had been my shepherd that night in the darkness, so Christ was his shepherd as he crossed the unknown span that we all will have to face one day.

17

DURING THE LOS Angeles Crusade, Bill and I were invited to Debbie Reynolds' home in Beverly Hills. It was to be an informal get-together around ten p.m.

Colleen Townsend Evans, a friend of Debbie's, had helped to arrange it. Debbie invited Billy Graham to meet several of her friends and the guest list included Glenn Ford, Edie Adams, Jack Lemmon and his beautiful wife Felicia Farr, and Mary Costa the opera singer. But the name on the list of invited guests that interested me the most was Judy Garland.

When we drove up the driveway to the impressive house, my thoughts basically were of Judy. I had been praying for her for a long time. She was a sensitive soul, caught in a treadmill that was not altogether her own making.

Her teens had been spent becoming a star tailored to the studio's wishes, and because of the tremendous stresses and strains the inevitable pep pills were used to get her going on the set. There was the insatiable craving deep within her to be loved and understood. Her attempted suicides had haunted me and I had so often prayed she would find the same answer I had found to my desperate search for peace.

When we walked into Debbie's "den", most of the guests had arrived. But Judy was missing. I was deeply disappointed.

After a while a discussion got going and one of the guests asked Billy Graham, "What *is* sin?"

Billy expounded at great length and I watched each face. They were all intent, listening.

As he spoke, I heard the door open and there was Judy standing—hesitating.

To see her face was quite a shock. Her eyes betrayed the years of agony she had gone through. This great performer had paid dearly for the joy she had given to so many.

She began to walk towards the couch that I was sitting on. I moved over and she sat down next to me. Whispering introductions, we then turned our attention to Billy Graham and listened as he told of God's inestimable love.

Suddenly Billy turned to me and said, "Joan, why don't you tell what has happened in your life?"

All faces turned towards me. Judy looked at me and smiled that beautiful smile as if in encouragement.

I began to tell of all my innermost fears and longings, my breakdowns and then my contemplated suicide. Of how the Lord had come in and given me hope where there had been nothing but despair and now I was assured of His love in my life.

After I finished speaking there was complete silence.

Then I felt a hand on my arm. It was Judy's.

"That was beautiful, darling. But you see—you had a need. I don't have any need."

Incredulously, I looked into her face remembering all she had been through. Perhaps there was no other person in Hollywood who had such a need as Judy, to be loved, to be needed. Not because of what she had achieved, but to be loved and understood for herself.

Maybe the many pills she had taken numbed her into this euphoria as they had done in my own life. It was only when I was alone and their effects wore off that I knew I had to find an answer to the constant gnawing deep within and the agonising loneliness.

When I read of Judy's death by a possible overdose, while she was living in London a few years later, I cried as if one of my own family had died, for I had walked the same horrendous path and but for His grace might have ended my life too.

I cannot judge her. I can remember that when I had taken my phenobarbital tablets, sometimes I would forget if I had had them and it was easy to take a second dose, and then a third, and then . . .

Judy heard of our heavenly Father's love that night and I do believe in a God who is ready to receive us, no matter how late.

Recently I learned that in the last few years of her life, Judy always carried a Bible with her wherever she travelled. It was the gift of a minister of whom she was very fond. Her favourite chapter was the love chapter in Corinthians in which Paul says: ". . . but love goes on forever . . ." (1 Corinthians 13 : 8.)

When I heard the news that Bill was to be sent to London to organise the Earl's Court Crusade there—I was overjoyed! To think of being able to live there with him and the boys! I could think of nothing more wonderful, because I could introduce them to so much that I loved in that city.

I have had an unashamed love affair with London ever since I can remember and my cousin Audrey's husband John once said to me, "When you die they'll probably find 'London' written on your heart."

Samuel Johnson had said, "When you are tired of London, you are tired of life."

After travelling all over the world there is still a magnetic quality about that city and I believe I shall never tire

146

of landing at Heathrow Airport and driving into London with all the anticipation and excitement that has always gripped me as soon as the plane touches down on British soil. Westminster Abbey, Buckingham Palace, the Tower of London are not mere tourist spots to me, they are part of my heritage and sometimes, in America, I just get homesick to walk down Piccadilly and take in all the sights and sounds that make up London.

We searched for some time to find accommodation. We finally found a little terraced house in Chelsea, and I fell in love with it instantly.

This house welcomed you as soon as you opened the front door, which had a large brass lion's head to greet you. It was decorated with antiques and the landlord, being an interior decorator, had bathed the walls in bright sunny colours: the combination was beautiful.

The boys had grown to admire and respect antiques, having an antique-mad mother, so I did not have to worry about them destroying the Regency fretwork tea table in the living room or the exquisite miniatures that hung in the bathroom. We learned to love this little house that only had two small rooms on each of its three floors. It had been built in the 1800s to accommodate the servants' families who worked in the large stately homes in nearby streets. Beneath us in a basement lived a lawyer and his mother, from Jamaica. We became close friends, which showed just how much love they must have had as we tramped over their heads all day.

It was delightful being able to entertain my family so often. Ann and Geraldine (my stepmother and half-sister) would come up from Eastbourne. My Aunt Hilda and cousin Audrey would join us and then in the evening my Uncle and Audrey's husband John would all stay for dinner. I felt very much like the "settled" housewife entertaining family and friends in my old country.

147

One day, not too long after moving into our little terraced house, I was reading to David as he lay in bed, suffering from measles. We heard the fire engines roar down our little street and come to a grinding halt outside our house. I looked out of the bedroom window and saw that the firemen were racing into the house next door, which had been made into apartments. Smoke was billowing out of the windows and I decided it was time to prepare for a quick evacuation if necessary. I bundled David up in some blankets and took him downstairs, waiting to see if we would have to leave. I felt the walls of our house. They were getting hot but the firemen soon put out the blaze and we were told there was no danger. We were so relieved.

Next day I read in the paper that the fire had happened in a flat belonging to Sarah Churchill. She was merely staying there while her new residence was being refurbished over at Eaton Square. I wrote her a little note saying how sorry I was to hear about the fire. To keep from appearing to push myself, I added that I did not like nosey neighbours, but knowing often there were crises that beset one to please feel free to call on us if we could be of any help. Back came a beautiful note thanking me and saying she hoped we would meet soon.

From there developed a very warm friendship with her and her surprise knocks on our front door heralded delightful hours spent talking over tea. I had loved her father so much and realised that the children of famous people often sacrifice tremendously as the world clamours for their attention. But she told of the warmth of this man who, though having to deal with the heavy burdens of state, loved to talk with her and there was a great bond between them.

One night she arrived on our doorstep asking if she could visit with her "angels" as she called Bill, and me. I told her if we were angels our haloes were mighty crooked! Not to be deterred, we talked for hours about the Lord we knew and she said she didn't want to "join" but she loved Him too. I explained that you didn't have to "join" anything but it was a question of giving yourself to this Christ and asking Him into your life.

Later she asked if she could go in and see the children sleeping in their bunk beds. Tenderly she touched them on their heads and as she bent over them her beautiful long red hair made me think how much she looked like Mary Magdalene. I remembered how much Jesus had loved her and thought how He loves Sarah who has experienced so much tragedy in her life.

If you have ever read any of her poetry you will understand so much about this woman, who reveals her feelings for the world to see the agonies she has known. Her ability to express herself is a great gift. To read her poetry is to weep with her—laugh with her and to know her feelings bared. Christ sees this lovely soul, understanding as no human can all that the heart is capable of bearing, alone. And yet not alone—for He is there!

These lines from Sarah's poem called "Loneliness" describe so vividly the torture that so many face each day:

> Loneliness
> Is the limit of your eye and feeling
> Loneliness is beyond safe horizons
> Loneliness is where there is no explanation
> No reason ever asked
> Loneliness is the stars
> The falling spaces
> Loneliness is a void on which
> You must force dimensions
> If you are to survive the endless years.

I feel such a tremendous affinity for Sarah—she has put into words what I had for so many years tried to do so often and failed miserably.

Often I would walk in Hyde Park, Kensington Gardens, and St James's Park, remembering how much had happened since I used to go there searching, trying to find an answer to the multitude of thoughts that flooded my brain. My life did have meaning now. A husband who loved me and was loved by me. We were complete opposites, yet we met each other's needs in so many ways. I had to come to grips with the realisation that Bill was not perfect and so had he with me. When we were first married, we had put each other on a pedestal and how quickly the pedestal cracked! Mine cracked a lot quicker than Bill's—it was made of a very cheap kind of clay! I had heard Archbishop Fulton Sheen once say on television that husbands and wives expected too much from each other. They were only the spark of love, but God was the flame and if we always looked to Him for our complete satisfaction in life we would never be disappointed with each other. This helped me so much. It is an illustration I have had to keep drawing on through my marriage, for the human in me has wanted perfection and demanded far too much of anyone.

Continuing to walk I would think of my other blessings—the boys. Both so different in temperament, but both so dear to me. They were such a handful while we were in London. David was six and Billy nine. It was perpetual motion from morning until night and the escapades never ceased. David was caught playing truant, having gone to Battersea Fun Fair for the day, complete with friend and cigars. Billy spent every available moment at the London Zoo and seemed to live in an animal world—his ambition then was to be a zoo keeper.

One day he decided to run away from home. He carefully

packed a small suitcase filled with his collection of miniature animals and determinedly strode out into the night. Five minutes later he returned announcing he would wait until after supper. We knew the call of food would be stronger than the call of the wild! After a good meal and some laughs with us he decided to postpone the venture indefinitely.

I loved them and their trust in me caused me to remember Jesus's words: "Except ye be converted and become as little children, ye cannot enter into the kingdom of heaven . . ." Matthew 18:3.

They did not question that we loved them and they simply expected to be fed and clothed. God had surely done that for me. The times I had questioned God's will in my life! There was a great deal of trial and error before I was convinced that His will was perfect. There would be clashes, and even today I still have to go on learning to say, "Not my will but Thine be done."

The meetings at Earl's Court went extremely well. The double-decker buses advertised "Billy's Back!" Everywhere people were talking about the Crusade, and it all brought back memories of Haringey, when I had sat there a spectator and gone home a partaker of His love and compassion.

I was counselling those who had come forward, helping them take their first few steps in the Christian life. I could not tell them that from now on they would have no more problems, for I had not experienced this and God had not promised it either. But I was able to tell them that over the years it had been His strength that had kept me. There are still times when I have completely messed up and failed those I love and the Lord. But He forgives and helps me over my frailties.

Oliver Goldsmith said: "Our greatest glory consists not

151

in never falling, but in rising every time we fall."

Many times it would be impossible for me to rise without the Lord. It reminds me of when the boys were learning to walk. They would do so well for a couple of steps and then crash—down they would go. Looking up to me or Bill they would seek our help to stand them up and then go precariously on their way learning to balance so that they could one day walk securely.

The night that stands out for me during the London Crusade was when my stepmother Ann and my sister Geraldine walked forward to give their lives to Christ. They had experienced such loneliness since the death of my father and I had prayed so much that they would come to know the full extent of His love.

"But my God shall supply all your need according to His riches in glory by Christ Jesus." Philippians 4 : 19.

At Earl's Court, I counselled many girls who felt their lives could never be changed, the same hopelessness pervading their thoughts as had filled my mind.

At the Crusade I was introduced to Rose (I have changed her name) while she was still under the influence of drugs. She was a frantic young girl of seventeen. Her dark hair was as wild as her eyes and she needed help desperately. The night before she had screamed out alone as in her drugged state she had hallucinated and felt and seen black spiders crawling all over her. I learned she had actively sold drugs in London at the age of fourteen, after running away from home. There was not too much of life that Rose had not experienced. Gradually I was able to win her confidence and I saw her begin to trust Jesus to help her.

I would meet her in Hyde Park and sitting by the Serpentine, watching the boats and the crowds who had come to relax in the sun, she would proceed to empty her handbag of its contents of drugs and say, in her Cockney voice:

" 'Ere Joan, you take 'em and get rid of 'em. I'm really trying to quit—honest I am."

I would take whatever she gave me and flush them down the toilet. One day however, I decided to keep a packet and take it to a meeting where I was speaking the next day. It would make a good illustration for me as I talked about the drugs that were destroying the young people's minds. As an afterthought I decided to get rid of the drug in the usual way and keep the silver foil it was wrapped in. I was so green! I could have easily been stopped and arrested for being in the possession of drugs. That next week a minister was arrested after showing his congregation from the pulpit a small package of marijuana.

But I was green too in my handling of Rose! She had told me she was on marijuana and hashish and here she had been giving me heroin. It was only when she gave me a hypodermic needle to get rid of I began to realise what was happening. Her brother had been hooked on heroin for some time.

Rose was completely uninhibited, especially if she were coming off a high. I remember walking in St James's Park with her, when suddenly she threw up her dress over her head and began scratching.

"Oooh, these mosquitoes are killing me!"

Two men in bowler hats passed us at the time, merely raising their eyebrows as they proceeded to walk along the path as if nothing had happened.

She would sometimes call in the middle of the night for help and Bill would go and get her, crumpled in a telephone booth, out cold. She finally went to live with a family in the country, who had a large house and even larger hearts. Here Rose began to feel she was wanted and understood. As time went on, she was able to quit the drugs and would come up to London to see us, her eyes not fogged over by the use of

153

them any more. She was bright and happy. The scars were still there and would always be, but Jesus had helped this girl who had been on the verge of destroying herself.

Rose had many problems—many highs and lows—and it was not an easy walk for her. She went on to help her brother and others find a way out of the destructive maze they had found themselves in.

During our stay in London, Bill and I visited my grandmother in hospital as often as we could. She had been ill for some time. It was heartbreaking to see her lying there with, it seemed, no purpose for living and no reassurance of a life to come.

Each time we would end our visit holding her hands and praying. There would always be the same reaction—a blank stare from Nanny and no comment whatsoever. I thought of the words she had said to me when I had explained what had happened in my life when Christ had come in and brought hope and His love.

"It's too late for me," she had said, "I'm too old to change."

On our way out past all the other white, sterile rooms with their elderly occupants, I would wonder, "Does she resent our prayers? Perhaps it would be better not to pray with her? Oh Lord, please don't let her die without knowing You!"

One day, I was in our bedroom in the little house in Chelsea, making the bed when it seemed the Lord said to me, "Today is the day. Ask Nanny again about Me!"

Quickly my mind raced—"I'll ask Bill to say something to her. After all, perhaps I'm too close to her. She knows too much about me as a child. She'll remember all my faults and perhaps they are what have stopped her from believing."

154

In the car on the way to the hospital, I confided my thoughts to Bill, glad to rid myself of any responsibility.

"No," he said, "you ask her. The Lord told you, not me, to do it."

I looked out of the corner of my eye, saw the set of his chin and knew—that was that.

Bill even waited outside the hospital in the car, so it meant I was completely alone. Only, not really. The Lord felt very close to me as I started to walk down the long corridors to Nanny's room.

Reaching it, I was told Nanny had worsened.

Walking into her private room, I saw her lying there small and helpless in the stark hospital bed. The room itself, devoid of any decoration, made her seem even more the poignant focal point of all attention.

"Nanny," I whispered and she opened her eyes and there was a slight flicker of recognition. I took her hand.

I remembered as I looked at that tired, work-worn hand how many times it had helped me over many heartaches. How many times I had held it as we had gone on so many adventures together as a child. I desperately wanted to convey to her my thanks and love for all she had ever done for me. Now the nurse had said it may not be long before the end.

"Dear Lord," I silently prayed, "please give me the right words to say."

Involuntarily it seemed I began to whisper to her, "Nanny, do you know that Jesus loves you?"

"Yes," she said very softly.

"And do you know He has a place waiting for you that is far more beautiful than anything you have ever seen?"

I told her there is a verse in the Bible that says: "For since the beginning of the world men have not heard, nor perceived by the ear, neither hath eye seen, O God, beside thee, what He hath prepared for him that waiteth for Him." (Isaiah 64:4.)

Her whole face lit up as she said, "Yes, I know!"

Her limp hand, that I was still holding pressed mine in silent affirmation. I looked into her face and Nanny never looked more beautiful to me for now there was an expression of joy and hope in her eyes.

I leaned over and kissed her and told her how much I loved her and that one day we would all be together again. She smiled and nodded.

My last memory of her is as I called, "Goodbye", at the door of her room, she waved to me and her face relayed the peace she had now found.

She died a few hours later. The nurse told us that after I had left, Nanny said to her, "I'm not afraid to die any more," and then slipped into a coma, from which she never awakened.

How thankful I was to the Lord that Nanny was with Him, suffering no more pain in a place that *was* far more beautiful than she had ever known.

The tears I shed were human ones as there was the natural grief of losing a loved one, but they were also tears of gratitude that she was with Christ and that we are never too old to find Him if we really want to.

18

TOWARDS THE END of our stay in London the days were marred by Bill's sudden haemorrhaging. I tried several times to get him to see a doctor but he insisted on waiting until we returned to the States in a month or so. Confiding in my London doctor, my fears grew as she told me just what to expect. The haemorrhaging stopped, but there were the nagging fears always in the back of my mind.

We settled into a rented house outside of New York City upon our return to the States. It was unfurnished, so we went to scores of house sales and bought the furniture piece by piece—hauling it ourselves. Even the Chinese Chippendale-style bedroom set that weighed a ton!

Gradually we assembled our finds. It was home once more. In a year we would have to dismantle everything and head on for fields unknown, so even though it was so temporary we tried to give the boys a feeling of security.

Bill had established an office in New York and commuted each day on the train. The boys were going to the local school and had made friends once more.

I was feeling very homesick for London with its instant transportation. "I'm not a suburban person, Lord, so why do I get stuck out here? It's all right for Bill. He goes into a city, establishes his office, and presto, he's running again. The boys go to their school and life seems to be the same for them; but here am I, stuck in the house when I could be out doing all kinds of things!" I bemoaned my fate of the suburban housewife, caught in the machinery of supermarkets, laundry, cleaning and cooking. The Lord had heard me talk like this before in other locations, so it was nothing new. Well, that was my lot and self-pityingly I gritted my teeth and acted out the part of the contented housewife—which I was not.

One morning something happened that made all my bemoanings fade into the background. I heard a cry from our room and running up the stairs I saw Bill, his face white and drawn. He had had a tremendous haemorrhage—far worse than before. Immediately I called a friend who recommended a doctor and Bill and I drove over as fast as we could. He was X-rayed and then came the interminable waiting for the result.

The phone rang while I was making the bed the next morning and the doctor's nurse was telling me Bill would have to call the office as soon as possible. Hesitatingly, I asked her if she could tell me anything.

After a pause she said, "There are lesions."

"Does that mean—" I hesitated forming the word—"cancer?"

"It could," she said.

My hands were a pool of sweat. I thanked her and hung up. The house seemed so empty—my whole world was crashing in on me as the sickening feeling of panic engulfed me. Me, who "died" inside every time Bill had to go on a trip. Now I was faced with the possibility of his having a major operation.

But I must not think of that—I had to keep control.

"Oh God, if only I could spare him all this!"

Just as so many times I had wanted to spare the children

hurts in their lives, I wanted to say, "No, there's been a mistake. These things happen to other people—not us."

I phoned Bill at his office and had to break the news to him. The silence as he let the news sink in made me want to cry out to him all my fears, but I asked the Lord for words of comfort. I found myself blurting out that it was going to be all right. God was going to take care of him.

He *did* take care of us, for on the very day Bill had to enter the hospital, Dorothy Williams arrived from England to stay in our home. She had been a medical missionary in Ghana for many years, and we had arranged for her to come over from England long before we knew of Bill's illness.

Early that morning we went to meet her ship in New York, having worked late into the night to get her room ready. The work was a blessed relief as Bill and I hung curtains, pictures, etc, and we tried to make it seem like home for her.

Always before when he had gone on trips my heart would ache as I packed for him. This time it seemed that every emotion I had been holding back would break into a torrent. There was so much I wanted to say to him—how much I loved him—how frightened I was. But I kept these feelings to myself as I asked the Lord for His restraint.

The time came for him to leave. We all went into the living room for prayer together. I do not know whose hand was shaking more as we all reached out for one another and prayed. The boys, not fully aware of all the implications, asked Jesus to take care of Dad and with complete faith that He would, kissed him goodbye.

Bill and I drove to the station where he was to get the train into New York City. We had agreed I would go in tomorrow early and be with him before the operation. We sat and waited together on the platform. I heard the train coming in the distance and hoped it would break down, but on came the roar as it belted down the track. As it screeched to a halt, I longed to be able to cry out "Don't go!"

"See you in the morning," I said, kissing him goodbye.

As I drove away I remembered that had been a line from the film *A Man Called Peter* when Peter Marshall was being taken to the hospital. They were the last words he ever said to his wife, Catherine. When Bill and I were first married, we had seen the film and we could not speak for some time afterwards, we had been so moved by this true story.

Now as I drove home the tears came tumbling down my face simply remembering all the happy times we had had together.

Arriving home, I managed to get to my room and shut the door. The floodgates broke and all my fears and longings were poured out to Christ. I could no longer hide my emotions.

I had to be strong. I was so weak. I had two boys who were depending on me.

Bill was depending on me too and all I wanted to do was run — run from this awful nightmare.

I didn't even know how to pray. Reaching for my Bible, I asked God to comfort me and give me His strength — I had none of my own.

Turning to Romans, chapter eight, my eyes fell on the twenty-sixth verse:

Likewise the Spirit also helpeth our infirmities: for we know not what we should pray for as we ought: but the Spirit itself maketh intercession for us with groanings which cannot be uttered.

In my despair it seemed God was showing me I did not have to be eloquent about my need. The groan that comes deep from the heart is understood by Him and there were many groans that night as I poured it all out, unashamedly. After a while I read from Matthew, chapter nine, where many of Jesus's healings are described. I came to the thirty-fifth verse:

And Jesus went about all the cities and villages teaching in their synagogues, and preaching the gospel of the kingdom, and healing every sickness and every disease among the people.

It was the words "every sickness—every disease" that made me feel a tremendous calm inside. Suddenly I felt His presence very strongly, as if His arms were encircling and strengthening me. Instantly I knew the Lord had given me this assurance and I believed from then on that Bill was going to be all right.

Bill called me from the hospital around nine o'clock and we prayed together. I felt so much stronger and now was able to tell him that the Lord had given me complete confidence about the outcome.

Next morning I awakened early and took the train into New York to be with Bill. As I entered the lift to go to Bill's room a sudden feeing of loneliness came over me.

"Oh Lord—if only someone from my family were with me . . ."

But again I sensed that I was not alone.

As the doors of the lift opened, I looked into the face of a dear friend of ours—Helen Stewart. She was the nurse who had recommended the doctor and she was caring for a patient on another floor. During a break, she had come up to see Bill and me. I knew the Lord sent her at such a time.

Bill looked so big and helpless lying in his hospital bed, but he was calm as we talked and prayed together.

The footsteps coming down the hall told us it was time

for his operation. Again the fears hit me and I asked the Lord to calm me.

Bill was given an injection and then very suddenly, after a quick "Au revoir" he was wheeled out and I was alone in the hospital room with the green walls overlooking New York City. There, where he had left them, were his slippers like two small islands—waiting.

I felt very tired and sat curled up in the armchair—all the sounds of New York and the hospital magnified along with the tense beating of my heart.

A nurse put her head around the door and asked if I would like a cup of tea.

Within minutes she was back handing me the much appreciated tea and told me to let her know if there was anything else she could do.

I thought of the words of Jesus, "If, as My representatives, you give even a cup of cold water to a little child, you will surely be rewarded." Matthew 10:42 *Living Bible.*

I felt very much like a small frightened child sitting there in that empty room and a simple act of giving me a cup of tea had reassured me again that He was with me. I don't remember the name of that nurse, but I will always remember and be grateful for her kindness.

Sitting there in that impersonal hospital room memories of our meeting flooded over me—our marriage and the happy years we shared.

After two hours, the doctor came to the room to tell me that Bill had come through the operation with flying colours. I was so thankful to him and the Lord.

"But," he said, "I am still not sure if I was able to remove all the tumour. It was the largest I have ever operated on."

My heart sank, but I found myself saying, "It's going to be all right. I know the Lord will heal him."

The doctor gave me a long look and then continued, "We

will know more in two days when we get the results from the lab. There may be wild cells."

Again I felt that dread go through me, but God had promised and I had to believe everything would be all right.

Bill finally came back to the room, very woozy but able to smile and say everything was fine. I sat holding his hand for as long as I could. I stayed in New York that night with Helen Stewart, exhausted and relieved that the operation was over.

The next day was spent with Bill, as he made a remarkable recovery. It was all the nurses and I could do to keep him in bed. However, always in the back of our minds was the result from the lab. Would it be a "pardon" or a sentence of death. God had promised a "pardon". My faith wavered at times, but only for moments for He had given me that incredible experience with Him at the house that night I had cried out to Him. I had to believe.

As I left Bill that night we again prayed together, remembering the result would be known tomorrow. There was not too much we could say audibly, but we felt the comfort of Christ once more.

I had arranged to take the hospital limousine as it would be very late when I finally arrived home.

It had already picked up six other passengers and I squeezed in between two ladies on the back seat. It was good to be able to relax and organise my thoughts before reaching home.

"Who is in that hospital?" said a strident voice.

I became aware of the elderly lady sitting to my left.

"My husband."

"He's going to die!" she said.

Shocked, I turned and looked at her and saw the face of a crone that would have been perfect type casting for a witch in *Macbeth*.

163

"He's not going to die," I heard myself say. "The Lord has promised that he is going to be completely healed."

"No," she cackled, "he is going to die. Prepare yourself. Do you have children?"

I nodded.

"Prepare them tonight. Tell them their father is going to die!"

The lady sitting on my right asked her to be quiet saying I did not need this kind of talk, but on she went getting louder and louder with her grim predictions. I sensed a terrible demonic presence in this woman and remembering Jesus's name was my defence, I kept talking of Him and His love and promises to me. It was as if I were listening to someone else as my voice kept repeating these assurances.

Finally, after what seemed hours to me but really had been about forty-five minutes, the car reached my house and I stumbled out the door with the old lady yelling after me, "Don't forget—prepare your children. He's going to die!"

I shall never forget the feeling that had swept over my whole body. As if I had been punched all over I managed to run up the front steps. Fumbling with my keys, the door finally swung open and the security of our home embraced me.

The boys were still up, waiting with Dorothy to hear all the news. Somehow I managed to talk to them coherently and then with a goodnight kiss and hug, they went to bed. A tremendous feeling of love for them swept over me. What a gift they were and at that moment I thanked the Lord again for the love that Bill and I had together and now was living on in them.

Dorothy had been holding the fort wonderfully and after she had told me all the news, I said goodnight and hastily ran up to the bedroom. Within the privacy of our room I put my head in the pillow and sobbed all the frightening experience of the woman in the car out to the Lord.

"God, You've promised in the Psalms that if I seek You, You will hear me and deliver me from all my fears. I can hear that woman's voice, see her face and I am terrified. Please give me Your peace again."

I lay there thinking of the fact that God's love did surround me and nothing could harm me. Finally exhausted, I fell into a fitful sleep remembering what I had to face tomorrow.

When I got back to the hospital Bill looked drawn and tired and he told me what a terrible time he had had after I left. Of how he had wrestled with such negative thoughts. His sister Madelaine had died of cancer at thirty-three. That haunted him. But then he opened his Bible to Proverbs 3:1, 2, "My son, forget not My law, but let thine heart keep My commandments; For *length of days, and long life*, and peace, shall they add to thee."

So often Christians dislike the Bible being used as an "instant survival kit" but, for the Browns, a verse has frequently been given just at the right time.

Looking back I can see how Satan used the old woman and Bill's frightening experience to try to make us doubt.

Finally the doctor arrived and told us the results of the tests. He was pretty certain Bill was going to be all right, but he would have to keep in close touch with him for a while to make certain everything was healing properly. Bill could leave the hospital in a few days. We were both delighted and thanked the quiet, dignified man who gave us such confidence.

Meeting him in the hall a few minutes later, he said to me, "He may have to come in again. There are some wild cells and I am concerned that they may flare up."

Once more I reiterated my belief that everything was going to be all right and thanked him for all he had done.

A few days later Bill came home. What a patient. Like a big old walrus squirming around in the confines of his bed. I remembered the time when he had had to go to the hospital in Miami with acute blood poisoning and the nurses were driven to distraction trying to keep his sheets in order. He was constantly on the phone organising the Crusade from his hospital room, twisting to and fro as he talked. Or else he would talk to the poor patient in the next bed who obviously longed for some peace! Now here he was at home, on the phone, twisting and turning, calling out instructions. But, oh, how good it was to have him home once more. I kept looking at him and thanking the Lord for sparing our dear one.

The next day I went to the supermarket to get some groceries. Upon my return, as my car pulled up alongside the house, a scene greeted my eyes that I could hardly believe. Bill was mowing the lawn! I jumped out and demanded he stop at once. "But honey, the grass really has grown so much . . ." I ordered him back to bed and without any hesitation called the doctor's office and "snitched" on him. The nurse was horrified and immediately told the doctor who prescribed some sedation for him.

Sedation does not work on Bill. Instead of quietening him down it seems to have the reverse effect and I can only say that when he decided to go into the office a week later just for a few hours, I did not argue. The peace was fantastic!

The time came quickly for Bill's first checkup and as we got ready to go into New York, thoughts began again to whirl around my brain. The old fears crept back.

"Wild cells" the doctor had said and this haunted me. We were a little late arriving for the appointment, so Bill asked me to go on up to the doctor's office while he found a parking space.

I opened the door and sat down in the waiting room, picking up a magazine that to me had no words or photographs as I idly turned the pages with my thoughts only on Bill. The doctor came out and seeing me said, "I'm glad you are here. I just want to warn you that Bill will probably have to go back into the hospital."

I shook my head, but did not say anything.

Bill arrived and went in for the examination. I started to shake uncontrollably with fear that swept over me and refused to diminish. Like a small child I wanted to find something to hold on to and I reached inside my handbag and saw my small red Bible. I pulled it out and began to read it. Again, as if the Lord knew how much I needed His comfort, the first verse I read was "This Man worketh miracles!" I whispered a silent "Thank you" and clung to that promise. Nothing had changed at all, just because Bill had to come and have a checkup.

After a while the door leading into the doctor's office opened and he came out to speak to me. "I've never seen a healing like this one. There isn't even a trace!"

I was so overwhelmed with joy I wanted to hug him, but the English in me decided it was not the proper thing to do at that moment. Bill emerged with a grin from ear to ear and thanking the doctor we raced out to the lift and decided to eat at our favourite Chinese restaurant to celebrate.

It has been over seven years now and each time Bill has gone back for a checkup he has thus far had a clean bill of health. We still get panicky around examination time. Bill especially has all kinds of thoughts swirling round, so much so that once on his way to the doctor's for his yearly checkup, he got a ticket for speeding; his thoughts were miles away!

We are among the fortunate ones who have experienced this. There are others who have found that the Lord has not answered their prayers in this way. If only there were a pat answer at times like these, but there isn't; and not until we

167

are face to face with Christ will we be able to understand why some are healed and others are not.

So often it is said "God makes no mistakes", but to the bereaved it lies superficially amongst the agony they have to bear. He doesn't make mistakes, even though I have often questioned in my own life why He chooses to take those who so often have so much to give this world. My little cousin Stewart, who died of leukemia, with his love of life and such a happy future ahead of him. Was it a mistake that God took him even before he had celebrated his sixth birthday? I believe if we only could understand all there is waiting for us when we die, we would confidently say "No mistake".

19

SOMETHING SEEMED TO be happening in our lives in the months that lay ahead. There would be a questioning as to whether the Lord wanted us to go on indefinitely, moving from city to city. The decision to conduct a Crusade in New York's Shea Stadium the year after Madison Square Garden meant we would have to move again even within the same city. Our lease was up and we had actually helped find the new tenants for our house—when we were told we would be staying on. Our landlords found us a one-bedroom flat in Bronxville and with the boys in the only bedroom (which became a den and dining room during the day), Bill and I shared the intended dining room as a bedroom. It measured nine feet by twelve and was a tight fit!

Bill told me he felt he was coming to the end of organising Crusades. I was really amazed as I had thought it would always be his life's work. He loved it and God had given him the gift of being able to organise masses of people and they responded eagerly to his leadership.

Each time we had had to move I had told the Lord that it was the last time, I just could not face travelling any more with a family.

But each time He would lovingly forgive the outbursts and give me His grace to go on. We had prayed so often about whether I should settle down with the boys somewhere and Bill continue to travel, but it would mean months and months of separation each year and always we felt the moving would be easier than the separation. So, even though I grumbled to the Lord, I thanked Him too that we could be together as much as possible.

Bill Junior was now entering high school and these years would be so important to him. In his fifteen years he had had twenty-one different homes and nine schools. He was gifted with being able to adapt very quickly to new surroundings and situations. But for David, it was different. Moving meant leaving friends and the familiar surroundings and it was hard on him. Once we arrived in a new city, however, he made friends very quickly but there was always the difficulty of adjusting to school.

Bill wrote a letter to Billy Graham telling him he felt he wanted to settle down. This would probably mean having to leave the organisation.

Many years before when we were temporarily settled in Washington, D.C. he had written a similar letter. Bill had been offered another position and seeing me so exhausted he had decided to write saying he would be leaving. As soon as it was mailed we realised it was written on emotion—not with the leading of the Lord. Imagine our surprise when our letter was returned by Billy's secretary, unopened. Her note with it said Dr Graham was out of the country for several weeks and since it was marked "Personal" she felt we would want to keep it until he got back. We thanked the Lord and tore up the letter.

This time however, we felt God was leading in our making a change.

Bill had to go to Plymouth, Massachusetts, to do the advance work for the 200th Anniversary Celebration at which Billy Graham would be speaking. I went up from New

York with him once or twice as this was my favourite part of the country. I felt so close to my English heritage and as a lover of history I took in all the historical sites. We started looking for a house in Plymouth and Bill had offers of work in Boston.

However, one day I was back in our little apartment in Bronxville when the telephone rang and I heard a voice saying,

"Hello Joan, this is Billy Graham."

I knew he must have received the letter by now and I groaned inwardly. Bill was up in Plymouth and here was I left to face the Chief! I stuttered and stammered—shades of Haringey once more—and there was Billy saying, "You can't leave. We need you. We want Bill out in California to run World Wide Pictures!"

Now I knew the Lord was making a big mistake. We had always said that California would be the last place we would want to raise our children, because it seemed there was no really settled family life there. I was rather inclined to agree with Mark Twain who once said, "California is a fine place to live—if you are an orange."

The constant sunshine would be wearisome to this British soul who had been bred on rain and fog! We just felt we would never want to live there permanently.

I have learned over the years that you never say "never" when the Lord is directing your life!

I told Billy Graham that Bill was in Plymouth and he said he would call him there. Many hours of prayer followed as I wondered just what our future held.

When Bill arrived home, one look in his eyes and I knew we would be leaving for California very shortly. Goodbye Plymouth. Goodbye to the old house that we looked at that had a spectacular view of Plymouth Harbour from the huge beamed den. Hello California and the wretched oranges. I had to make a big adjustment and I had to make it fast!

Bill and I flew out to California and in three days, after looking at many houses without an ounce of character, we found a little red barn, a copy of a New England farm house. The Lord was giving me a touch of my favourite area of the country after all. Its beams and brick fireplace mesmerised us and we fell in love with it immediately. (We were to find it had many flaws, but those beams kept us looking up!)

We flew back to New York to pack our belongings and collect the boys. Moving day came. When it was time to leave I went into Billy and David's room and there David sat in a corner, tears rolling down his face as he read a folder of letters his class had written to him. They were farewell letters and when I started to read them, I sat down with him and bawled too. We prayed together and asked God to bless his friends and thanked Him for them. We asked that He would go before us in our travels to California and that He would have friends waiting for David there. He was to answer our prayers abundantly.

In all the times of questioning as I packed, there had been two verses that had stuck in my mind and would not leave:

"He led them forth by the right way, that they might go to a city of habitation" (Psalm 107:7) and ". . . all thy children shall be taught of the Lord; and great shall be the peace of thy children" (Isaiah 54:13).

I felt a great peace as we left New York, knowing that God had led us the right way and had promised to take care of our children.

California has proved to be a wonderful home. Family life is what you make it wherever you are. The years we have spent in our house have been exceedingly happy ones and it has been good to see my children have roots. Of course, there have been the agonies of the teen years—it seems no one can escape their torments and always I have made myself remember what I went through as a teenager, when dealing with many crisis situations. If it were not for the knowledge that I could pour out all my hopes and fears to the Lord on behalf of my children, I know I would have given up years ago. There is a tremendous pull outside the home calling to these adventurous souls and if my knees are calloused, there are very good reasons! Each time they leave the house I try to remember to pray that His loving protection will go with them. I am very proud of my two sons who love life and are not afraid to meet it head on.

Once we were settled in our house with all the treasures we had collected from around the world, I enjoyed seeing it begin to be a home. Only two months went by and one night I surveyed it lovingly, having spent most of the day polishing the floors until the whole place shone. I decided we were indeed "settled". Bill came home for dinner and remarked how great everything looked.

Next morning at precisely six o'clock we were awakened by a huge jolting sensation. Our house felt as if it was about to be swept down the hill. A large wall mirror fell on to our bed, just missing Bill, and the noise of china and glass smashing through the house made me realise—an earthquake! I fought to get out of bed as it rocked convulsively and I managed to get to David's room. Bill Junior had practically fallen down the stairs from his attic bedroom and we all huddled, waiting in the hallway to be certain the 'quake was finished. It was pitch dark and no one could find anything when the shaking finally stopped. I could not find a pair of shoes that matched—Bill Junior couldn't even find his trousers! We were all running around trying to get dressed before another one hit. Finally we got organised and the morning light began to show us the extent of the damage—$4,500 worth.

The floors I had taken so long to polish were now covered in glass and broken china—many of my antique plates which

I had brought back from England were broken and had dug into the boards. Books were everywhere as shelves had come down and when I opened the larder, where I kept the food, a sight greeted me that was beyond description. Treacle was oozing over everything as it lay piled on the floor. I shut the door and decided to worry about that lot later!

My first reaction was of thankfulness that none of us were hurt. We could so easily have been injured. Our house was a mess, but we were untouched. I thanked God.

My second reaction was plain annoyance. Here we were supposed to be settled down at last and now look at this mess! Bill Junior was furious as all his intricately-made models had been broken and he kept saying, "I'm going to sue. I'm going to sue."

When asked just who, he said he did not know but he'd find out and man, would he ever sue!

Bill went off on a filming assignment. The boys went to survey the San Fernando Valley and I was left to clear up the mess, muttering about it being a man's world.

The eeriness that pervaded the area after it was over is something I shall never forget. There was no electricity, no gas and the water was filled with mud. All over the Valley small fires could be seen. I could not help but think of how at a time like this we are totally in God's hands and our only security is in Him. Our lives are always dependent on Him, but sometimes it takes an earthquake to realise how vulnerable we are.

With Bill's work, it now meant he would leave us quite often to go with the film crew to different states and countries and I found the separation very hard.

Each time I had to pack for Bill, fears swept over me. Just the sight of that suitcase would send my thoughts racing —"What if something happens to him? I dread the thought of being without him, even for a few weeks!"'

Then he would be gone and I would be left with the terrible ache inside me that seemed to drain all my energy.

During a time of separation, I read a letter that Dietrich Bonhoeffer, the theologian, had written while he was imprisoned by the Nazis. In it he told of the unutterable agony of separation and the longing that was so deep it made him sick. He went on to say:

It is nonsense to say God fills the gap; He does not fill it, but keeps it empty so that our communion with another may be kept alive, even at the cost of pain . . . The dearer and richer our memories, the more difficult the separation . . . From the moment we awake until we fall asleep we must commend our loved ones wholly and unreservedly to God, and leave them in His hands, transforming our anxiety for them into prayers on their behalf.

Reading this I began to realise that all the energy I had exerted fretting and being concerned could be turned into a positive force by my prayers. I had prayed for Bill before, but the Lord was showing me that the joys of deeper prayer life with Him could only come about as I turned the ache inside into a time when my attention could be devoted specifically to the one I loved in Christ.

I began working as a volunteer with the wives and mothers of Prisoners of War of North Viet Nam. God used the ache in my heart to help me empathise with these courageous women and I could only point them to Jesus as the terrible weeks of waiting turned into years. For some there was the joy of reunion—for others the knowledge that their loved one was dead—and yet others with the news that theirs were still missing in action.

Recently when Bill and I were discussing with Bill Junior his future and our concern for him, he looked us right in the eye and said, "Don't worry about me, Mom and Dad, I know Who I belong to and I know where I'm going." They were words I wish that every parent could hear and we both were so grateful to the Lord for this assurance coming from our son's lips.

While attending college, Bill Junior has been driving an ambulance. His experiences have made a man out of him in a very few months. One morning he came home after having worked all night as part of his training in the emergency room of St Joseph's Hospital in Burbank. He was weary but I could tell he did not feel he had worked in vain. There had been so many emergencies that night, he said, but one had stood out in his mind above all the others. An epileptic had been brought in who had tried to commit suicide. Bill worked on him for hours, holding him while he would go into violent fits. During this time, he was able to talk to and comfort this distraught man who had felt life was not worth living anymore because of his illness. Bill spoke about the Lord to him and as the man was wheeled out to be taken to a room in the hospital, he said to Bill, "You've got God in you—don't let anyone take Him away."

After Bill Junior finished telling me this story I thought of the many times when Bill and I wondered if any of our spiritual training had rubbed off on our children. I was glad some had and was reminded again of Ruth Graham's statement, "You should never judge a painting until the artist is finished with it."

The telephone rang one morning which had started out as a routine day. Answering it, I heard Frank Jacobson's voice. He is vice-president of World Wide Pictures and he and his wife Dorothy have been friends of ours ever since we first were married.

"Joan," he said, "how would you like to play Fran Cole, the mother, in *Time to Run*?"

I was speechless as I listened to him telling me that he

and Jimmy Collier, who was to direct the film, had been discussing the idea of my playing the part. Naturally I was excited and said that I would love to be able to appear in a film again.

A feeling of joy came over me. I could hardly wait to tell someone. Bill came home for lunch unexpectedly that day and I raced to the back door to tell him the news.

"Oh, my," he said, "I don't know whether that is a good idea or not. People are going to say it is nepotism—my heading the studios. I shall really have to think about that!"

My balloon was a little deflated but still riding high. Bill Junior was next to come home and when I told him the news he said, "Wow, after all these years of not acting—that may be a real bomb with you in it, Mother!"

Two down and one to go—I was really relying on David to say something positive. I heard him whistling as he came up the hill to our back door and I hastily opened it and told him the news.

His face lit up—"Congratulations, Mom—let's celebrate!"

("Thank you Lord for David." He had given me the boost and the assurance I needed.)

Jimmy Collier, as we discussed the part, said to me, "You'll really have to do your homework, Joan. All eyes will be on you when you come on that set. As the wife of the president of World Wide Pictures, you are going to have to prove you can really do this part."

My legs were like jelly when the morning arrived that heralded my first day's shooting, and if it hadn't been for the Lord I would have run for the nearest exit!

As the weeks proceeded the cast and crew were wonderful to me. Jimmy gave me the confidence I needed as he quietly whispered directions.

Randy Carver, who played my son and whose character

177

was the main one in *Time to Run*, became like a real son. Together with his girl friend in the film, played by Barbara Siegel, we had many enjoyable times together.

Ed Nelson, who many remember as Dr Rossi in *Peyton Place* or in films like *Airport '75*, played my husband, and proved to be a great help. He told me that if only one life was helped through the film he felt it was worth more than anything he had ever done. More than 500,000 decisions for Christ have been made through *Time to Run*.

Families are reunited as they watch the story that touches their own lives. In preparing for my part I could only imagine what it would be like if Billy or David had run away from home—the heartache would be unbearable and this woman Fran Cole did not have Christ to help her. I looked at this woman who had nowhere to turn and I really asked the Lord to help me portray her so that women sitting in the audience could identify with this person.

I toured for a while with the film as it premièred and was overwhelmed many times as I saw God use it. One night I was standing at the back of the auditorium watching the ending of the film. A young teenaged girl spotted me and flung her arms around me, crying. "Thank you, oh thank you so much—you remind me of my own mother."

Then she was gone. I was deeply touched.

My heart has been burdened for today's young people, especially when I read the frightening statistics that coldly announce the numbers that take their own lives. Suicide is the third greatest killer on the college campuses today.

"It's empty, life is empty," they cry.

If only they could see Jesus wanting to love them, not for what they have achieved, but loving them in the purest sense —unconditionally.

There were many instances of seeing people's gratitude for a film that brought them to Christ. My Alexandrite ring

178

to this day bears the marks of a man's hand as he shook mine expressing his thankfulness for what *Time to Run* had done in his life. While telling me that he now understood his responsibility to his son, he did not realise that his hand had grasped mine so tightly my ring had been crushed. I had it straightened afterwards but it has never been quite the same. But each time I look at it, I am reminded of a man whose life was changed; through Christ he has a deeper understanding of what he should be as a father.

The most meaningful showing of the film for me was when I was able to go to London where, in a small theatre, Bill and I invited many of the people who had had such an important part in my life.

The people attending depicted to me a composite of the years that had gone before. There was my Headmistress from school days who had faithfully taught me the Scriptures and introduced me to the same Jesus who had to wait for me to follow my heart's desires before I came to a realisation that He was all I had been seeking. Joy Rayner who had been a friend at school and had dared me to ask for an autograph which had meant the beginning of my stage career. Then much later her cousin who had taken me to hear Billy Graham. There were friends from when I worked in an office dreaming of days ahead that would bring me fame on the stage. Then too there were so many who had helped me in my Christian walk when I needed so much love and understanding. Rose was there who had been so caught up in the terrible web of drugs. She was hugging me and telling me Jesus was still O.K. as far as she was concerned.

I looked at my family sitting there—my stepmother Ann and my sister Geraldine, my Aunt and Uncle and my cousin Audrey and her husband John. I remembered the years they had to face watching me go on so blindly. There had been many agonies and very few ecstasies. Now as I spoke to them all, I hoped I could convey my happiness in Christ.

As the film was shown, I sat there very conscious that two other people with whom I had shared Jesus could not be there, my father and my grandmother. But they were with Him and in the darkness of the theatre I was grateful.

20

IN WRITING, I have had to go back into the past and delve into the recesses of my mind, finding incidents that had long been put aside—hopefully forgotten. It has often been painful. Without Christ this would be an empty story of someone still searching, questioning her life. It would be full of meaningless anecdotes, with the heart of it missing.

I have not arrived. There is still so much to learn. But by loving Christ and being loved by Him I am now able to reach out to those who are still seeking and say "Look what I have found—food for the hunger that gnaws within our souls!"

Our past, our childhood, dominates our future years. It moulds how we react to certain situations, our ability to reach out to others. But we cannot lean on our past. The past should be used to learn from—but not to tear us down. All we confess to the Lord is forgiven and forgotten just as David said in the Psalms:

"As far as the east is from the west, so far hath he removed our transgressions from us. Like a father pitieth His children, so the Lord pitieth them that fear Him. For He knoweth our frame . . ." Psalm 102:12–14.

Those last five words have been repeated by me over and over again when stress has made me feel as if I were going to break again. With a heart cry to God I have thanked Him that He is with me and does know the extent to which this frame can be bent but not broken. I need to have His resiliency in my life so that the branches of my mind will not snap when the times come that make life difficult to bear.

Through the Psalms we are able to come to the place where we no longer need to feel guilty for all the impassioned feelings that so often sweep over us. When David wrote those masterpieces he was setting a pattern that all who have suffered torments of the mind could look to and find comfort. He knew the deepest valleys and was not afraid to tell God the truth about himself.

If we were always on a mountain top we would miss what God has been able to teach us in the valleys—that He is always with us, even on days when we feel He is unreachable. It is at this time I have to rely completely on my faith and say—"Lord, I do not feel your presence with me, but I know that You *are* there and this wilderness is only temporary in my life."

Moments of doubt have often caused interruption of communication. As if God knew there would be these times, Jesus's encounter with the distraught father who sought healing for his child in the Gospel of Mark shows us these are normal feelings.

"Jesus said unto him, if thou canst believe, all things are possible to him that believeth. And straightaway the father of the child cried out and said, with tears, Lord I believe, help thou mine unbelief!"

I have cried out to God my unbelief and always there has come a peace that is not complacent but one that is God's. It is not of my own making, for then all I would have in my life would be a feeling of smug satisfaction. I am a weak woman—but I have a strong God.

Recently in a women's magazine I was saddened to read

a statement by a well-known actress who said she despised people who crack under strain. Shakespeare put it very succinctly when he said, "He jests at scars that never felt a wound."

Those who have never been wounded by the agonies of the mind can never fully understand the tortures that so many go through. But I know this: God understands, for in His life here on earth Jesus never mocked or belittled those who were weak either in mind or body. He left His scorn for those who felt better than others.

We are all made differently. We are all born with a distinct personality. No two fingerprints are alike and this is what comforts me and makes me realise even more that a God who has taken the time to attend to these minute details cares deeply for the individual He has created. Cares for all the happenings in our lives, however small or insignificant.

During a visit to a jail in Honolulu where I was allowed to talk to some of the girls, I met a young prisoner whose eyes showed she was scared to death.

She had come into the room where I was to speak, in her shapeless prison dress, with thongs on her feet that did not fit properly, smoking a cigarette. She sat down and seemed unapproachable.

A few scenes from *Time to Run* were shown and then I spoke briefly about the forgiveness of Christ in my life. I told of the love that was waiting if only we would receive it. Then I asked if we could pray together.

When I looked up, the girl with the scared eyes was crying.

"Pat," I said, "can I help you in any way?"

"No, there's no hope for me. I've known about God, but I have failed Him so terribly. There's nothing anyone can do."

Gradually she told me this story. She was the granddaughter of a minister and she knew all about the Bible, but felt there was no forgiveness left for her. I turned to 1 John

1 : 9 and quickly she said, "I know that verse—that won't help me!"

But I read it to her anyway.

"If we confess our sins, He is faithful and just to forgive us our sins and to cleanse us from all unrighteousness."

"Pat, don't you see God is saying He will forgive ALL unrighteousness?"

She looked at the verse, then up at me.

"I've never thought about that word 'all'."

We talked for a while and I began to see a change in her face as she realised there was still hope for her. *All* unrighteousness meant *every* unrighteousness and she prayed with me that Christ would come in and forgive everything in her life. As she looked up, there were still tears in her eyes, but this time I could see she had reached out and grasped hope from our Saviour.

Pat still had to face trial, possible extradition and a long separation from her little girl whom she adored. We hugged as I left and I promised to keep in touch with her. Next day I was allowed to telephone the jail to find out how she was. She told me that Jesus had been so real to her and now no matter what she had to face she knew it would not be alone.

Over the months I wrote to her and received the most wonderful letters. She was extradited to the mainland and was sentenced to serve two years in the Women's Penitentiary. She knew she had to pay for her crime and accepted her sentence, bearing the heartache of being parted from her little girl. Her letters arrived regularly and always they were filled with words of God's love for her. One letter told of an incident that had distressed her:

It is pretty rough here. A matron had bleach thrown in her face and was blinded. I have my ups and downs, but I am hanging on tight to Christ. I know He is the only way to eternal happiness and through Him all things will eventually work out. I'll eventually be free to provide a Christian home for my daughter.

Pat helped others in the penitentiary to find Christ and even when at first her parole was turned down, she took it bravely.

The same day I signed the contract to write this book I received a letter from Pat. It contained the news both of us had been praying for:

Dear Joan, I have good news! The board gave me my freedom yesterday! I'm going home! I'm free! I want to write and tell everyone that I'm FREE!

To this day I do not know what her crime was. I never asked. I only saw her as a person like myself who needed the forgiveness of Christ and the hope that He alone could give.

This is the reason I have wanted to write this book. Like Pat I want to tell everyone that I too am free! Free from the prison that had invisible bars, for it was a prison within my mind and soul.

"If the Son therefore shall make you free, ye shall be free indeed." John 8:36.

We make our own prisons when we shut out God. I am no longer bound but free, free to worship Him and there are days when I feel I can reach out and touch the very heights of heaven as I find such consolation in the knowledge of His love.

Among my memorabilia is a letter that for years has meant a great deal to me. It is dated September 25, 1957. Here is an excerpt from it, written by Mrs J. Edwin Orr, Port Shepstone, South Africa, to Mrs Ruth Graham.

You know when Edwin was in a very remote part of New South Wales, more than 500 miles from Sydney, a man approached him. He told Edwin an amazing story and I knew you'd be interested.

He said he'd been looking at an Australian picture magazine more than four years before and his eye was attracted to a photo of an actress. Having nothing to do with the movies, he was not impressed, but a strange conviction from the Spirit burdened him to pray for her conversion. He personally felt it was a waste of time, nevertheless, he kept praying for the girl. In 1954, the burden lifted, as if the Lord said, "You need not carry this burden any longer." He had no idea whether the girl died or was truly converted, for he had never heard of anyone in the movies being converted. But he remembered her name—Joan Winmill—and when Edwin checked dates with him he found that the burden had lifted during the Haringey Crusade, when you were actually helping Joan! The man's name is Ellwood Fischer and he is a great man of prayer. Naturally, he was greatly encouraged to learn of Joan Winmill's conversion. Knowing that you must be in touch with Joan, I thought you might wish to tell her how a stranger in far-off Australia prayed so long for her conversion.

If I ever needed proof that God answers prayers, this letter is emblazoned on my heart as evidence. While I was alone, without hope, in my flat in London crying out to Him, a man many thousands of miles away in Australia was touched by the Spirit to pray for me.

I will praise the Lord no matter what happens. I will constantly speak of His glories and grace. I will boast of

186

all His kindness to me. Let all who are discouraged take heart. Let us praise the Lord together, and exalt His name.

For I cried to Him and He answered me! He freed me from all my fears. Psalm 34:1–4.